THE ARAB MIDDLE EAST

and

MUSLIM AFRICA

THE INSTITUTE OF ETHNIC STUDIES was established at Georgetown University, Washington, D. C., for the study of the history and culture (secular and religious), the economic, political and social development, the racial and linguistic characteristics

a) of the nations and peoples forcefully submerged in the Soviet-Russian Communist-dominated orbit

and

b) of the peoples who are emerging from their former colonial status and are securing their national independence.

It is the aim of the Institute to publish the results of its studies in order to disseminate better knowledge and deeper understanding of these problems, and thus further the cause of just and lasting peace among nations.

EXECUTIVE DIRECTOR

Tibor Kerekes

STAFF

George C. A. Boehrer
Tennyson Po-Hsun Chang
Jules Davids
Roman Debicki
Lev Dobriansky

Jan Karski
Charles Schertenleib
Hisham Sharabi
Olgerd Sherbowitz-Wetzor
Cyril Toumanoff

Cyril A. Zebot

Members of the Faculty of Georgetown University

The Arab Middle East

and

Muslim Africa

Edited by

Tibor Kerekes, Director

THE INSTITUTE OF ETHNIC STUDIES
GEORGETOWN UNIVERSITY,
WASHINGTON, D. C.

FREDERICK A. PRAEGER, *Publishers*
NEW YORK

BOOKS THAT MATTER

First published in the United States of America in 1961
by Frederick A. Praeger, Inc., Publishers
64 University Place, New York 3, N. Y.

© 1961 by the Institute of Ethnic Studies,
Georgetown University, Washington, D. C.

Library of Congress catalog card number 61-8215
Printed in the United States of America

Preface

The seven studies composing this volume were originally presented by the authors at the Third Annual Roundtable Conference of the Georgetown University's Institute of Ethnic Studies.

The Conference, held on April 29 and 30 of this year, was devoted to an analysis and interpretation of the developments and issues which profoundly affected the Arab Middle East and Muslim Africa. It dealt with the mighty force of Islam and the many and vehement challenges to which it is now exposed; it treated of the truly revolutionary, political, social and economic changes that occurred in the Arab Middle East during the last decade; it dealt with the new intellectual and cultural attitudes of the young Arab generation; it analyzed the problem of awakened national consciousness of Islamic Africa and posed the question of whether it will replace Islam as the unifying principle of the many regions of tropical Africa; and finally it investigated the prospects of a United Maghrib, i.e., the chances of a union of Tunisia, Algeria and Morocco.

As director of the Institute and editor of its publications, I wish to thank the authors for their penetrating contributions, the President and Directors of Georgetown University for their interest in and support of the Institute, my colleagues on the Staff for their voluntary services, the Annual Giving Fund of Georgetown University for the generous grant, and the Publisher for sharing this venture.

TIBOR KEREKES

Washington, D.C.
August, 1960

Contents

Preface

ISLAM IN THE MODERN WORLD   9
Hamilton A. R. Gibb

A DECADE OF REVOLUTION: POLITICAL AND
SOCIAL CHANGES, 1949-1959   27
George F. Hourani

POLITICAL AND INTELLECTUAL ATTITUDES
OF THE YOUNG ARAB GENERATION   47
Hisham Sharabi

ISLAM AND NATIONALISM IN AFRICA   63
William H. Lewis

PROSPECTS FOR A UNITED MAGHRIB   85
William Sands

PATTERNS OF RECENT ECONOMIC DEVELOP-
MENT IN THE ARAB STATES   95
Albert J. Meyer

GENERATIONS, CLASSES AND POLITICS,
1952-1959   105
William R. Polk

Index of Names and Places   121

Islam
in the
Modern World

by

Hamilton A. R. Gibb

Hamilton A. R. Gibb, formerly Laudian Professor of Arabic at Oxford University, is
University Professor and J. R. Jewett Professor of Arabic at Harvard University and
also Director of its Center for Middle Eastern
Studies.

1

The term *Islam* is ambiguous in common usage. It can be imagined by a triangle; the three angles are a doctrine, a culture, and a history, and the three sides enclose a community. The triangle may change its shape, it may be smaller or larger, the size of the angles may vary in relation to one another; but the community always remains enclosed within them. To renounce any one of them is to renounce them all, to step outside the boundary lines, to cease to belong to the community. Since this structure is set within the flux of the terrestrial world, it has had to meet a succession of challenges which, focussing attack on one angle or the other, have threatened its integrity. It has now to meet the challenges of the modern world. These certainly differ from the earlier challenges in multiplicity, density and violence; but whether their combined assault will break through from without or burst open the boundaries of the triangle from within still remains to be seen.

Every challenge in the past has called out two opposed reactions. One, the negative, has insisted that the angles and boundary lines are fixed—that doctrine, cultural determinants and historical components, defined "as of now," can admit of no modification. The other, the positive, has striven to incorporate new insights and new experiences, even when they ran counter to the ideas "as of now." The second, positive, reaction has almost always been successful in the long run, but only by so adapting and reshaping the new elements that they could eventually be fitted into the structure without unendurable contradiction and violence. Thus, in the past, there has been a slow but persistent modification and redefinition of the content and connotation of Islamic culture, Islamic history, and even (although to less extent) of Islamic doctrine, usually by processes of quiet and informal pressures operating within the community. Since the problem of Islam in the modern world is the result of challenges of unprecedented violence to all its angles at once, it is obvious that the subject as a whole is too vast to be treated in this short study. I shall leave aside therefore, the political, economic and social facets of the problem, and concentrate on the modern challenge to Islam as a religion, in the wider sense. Even so, I can do little more than suggest themes for examination, rather than aim to supply solutions.

2

We shall approach our subject first from the outside, and outline the means by which the triangle was constructed and maintained. Most of us are fully aware of the central importance of the community in Muslim thought. It can be said with much truth that the major concern of religious scholarship, devotion and activity in Islam has been the effort to promote the spiritual and moral unity of all Muslims everywhere. This was no easy task, in view of the great variety of races and cultural traditions that were being continually absorbed into Islam. Inevitably, then, the approaches of Muslim thought to each of the major constituents of the community—those three angles of the triangle —were governed by the imperative needs of the community-as-unity rather than by more abstract general considerations.

In the field of doctrine, Islam had only one serious challenge to meet, that of the Hellenizing so-called rationalists, who attempted to objectivate (to anticipate a term that I shall be using later) the concept of God by defining it in intellectual categories and thereby, of course, confining God within their limits. This ran so deeply against the grain of Muslim feeling and conviction that it was eventually squeezed out, leaving as its legacy not a metaphysic, but only a formal theology which asserted the sovereignty of God, intact and unexplicated, and therefore beyond doctrinal discussion and dissension.

In the field of culture, the chief concern of the religious leaders was to work out first the principles, and then the details, of a uniform system of ritual and law, the *Sharī'a*, to supersede all previous laws and usages. Backed by the authority of divine revelation in the Qur'an and the example of the Prophet Muhammad, this should (and did) supply an infallible guide, to be gradually adopted by all sections of the community for the conduct of its spiritual and social life. Then, at a later stage, the religious leadership set itself to capture all forms and expressions of intellectual activity and to channel them into conformity with the central religious concepts, by carefully pruning away everything that smelled of heterodoxy or suggested too free a spirit of enquiry. So philosophy was de-Hellenized and pressed (rather superfluously) into the service of theology, and in the hands of the Sufi poets popular love lyrics and drinking songs were transformed into vehicles of mystical imagery.

In the field of history, the scholars would seem to have had a particularly arduous task, since much of Islamic history (as of other history) in the political sense is far from being conspicuously edifying. But they had an acceptable solution at hand. For them, Islamic history is not political history as such, but the history of the community, in relation to which the rise and fall of political organisms is largely incidental. It is contained in the immense series of many-volumed biographical dictionaries which have been composed from the earliest centuries of Islam down to the present day, and which document the uninterrupted transmission of the Muslim heritage in all branches of learning and all lands by countless men and women. Political history was, as

it were, redeemed from sterility and corruption only in the measure that the political rulers furthered and protected the labors
of these transmitters.

3

Of these fields, however, it was the second, and especially the
study and furtherance of the *Sharī'a*, the Sacred Law, that con-
stituted the kernel of formal religious activity; and to this intense
concentration on the *Sharī'a* is mainly due the really remarkable
consistency of the Muslim community down to the present
century (notwithstanding all the minor varieties of regional
practice), and the scarcely less remarkable social equilibrium
within and between different regional and economic groups.

Nevertheless, this outward balance and consistency concealed
an inner division which the religious leaders, in spite of strenuous
efforts, never succeeded in overcoming. In the political institutions, the governing classes had for centuries adopted and followed a system of political ethics derived from the old imperial
traditions of Western Asia, and very far removed indeed from
the Islamic ethical values. To speak bluntly, those vices which
the Muslim critic never wearies of castigating in the Western
world under the heading of "materialism" were solidly rooted
long before the nineteenth century among the governing classes
in the Islamic world, and had no small number of practitioners
in the so-called middle classes as well, among the men of busi-
ness, and even among the representatives of the Sacred Law itself.

4

"Materialism" is thus no new thing in Islamic society. Its
apparent expansion in the modern world can be regarded as a
function of several factors: 1) that the social controls formerly
imposed on its public expression have largely been removed; 2)

the continuous enlargement of the middle classes or bourgeoisie has widened the social circles within which materialist values tend to prevail; 3) most of the materials, printed, oral, visual, by which Muslims communicate with one another and with the outer world emanate from these circles, and the image presented by them is a composite which reflects their values; 4) the direct and indirect impacts and influences from the West—literary, political, technical, etc.—reinforce the concentration of public attention upon material objects and ends.

The total result of this process has been to increase immensely the element of objectivation in the political, social and economic life of the Muslim community as a whole (objectivation meaning the assignment of positive and self-validating values to actions, institutions, etc., in themselves). All this has necessarily reacted on both the concept of Islam and its traditional realizations in terms of specific attitudes and institutions. But the problem remains—how to measure these changes, how to relate them to the inner reality of Islam as a religion. And here our techniques of measurement, derived from the experience of our Western societies, may lead us astray, unless we can adjust them to the different coordinates of the Eastern societies.

5

Materialism, while it contaminates the practice of religion, does not destroy religion until it becomes secularism, i.e., rejection of the basic postulates of religious thought. And this is less easy in Islam than in our modern Western world. The ethics and practice of materialism may be much the same in both, but secularism carries vastly different connotations, means very different things, in Western and Muslim thought. Secularism in the West is essentially a view of the world or universe and everything in them as governed by iron law or necessity, and of all systems of morality as relativist, as expressions of the collective experience of different societies, or the mores of particular groups, or of a utilitarian or empirical philosophy. There may still be "mystery" in the universe, as well as in human life, but "mystery" means only natural processes whose character, structure and operation have not yet been discovered by objective experiment. Rationality is the recognition of the necessary character of law, and rational action is the calculus of processes to produce results in conformity with given laws.

The Islamic world, indeed the Orient in general, has never accepted such a concept of law, with its corollary of material objectivation. The failure to realize this fact and its consequences has probably been the greatest obstacle to our understanding of Islam. Little by little, however, those Western observers who have acquired, by sympathetic intuition, the power to penetrate more profoundly into Muslim psychology, and among whom I may mention especially Louis Massignon, have begun to show us where the source of our error lies.

When the Muslim accuses the West of materialism, he does not mean merely that the West is interested only in the material goods and conditions of life. He means that the thinking of the Westerner is conditioned throughout by objectivations deriving from a basic dualism, of which precisely the concept of all physical action as governed by impersonal necessary law is a typical example. The specific characteristic of Muslim mentality (I must add that here I speak more particularly of Arabs and Persians) is the *primacy of symbol over object*. Not that the object is disregarded, but it inheres in the symbol; it is *there,* whether or not it is "objectivated" in our sense. When we translate the Arabic term *al-haqq* by "the truth" or "the right," we are not wrong in the linguistic sense, but we are objectivating the Muslim connotation of "that which truly *is*." The function of action in the social or personal sense is to conform to "that which truly *is*," not by way of its objective realization, but rather that the subjective doing fuses with the process inherent in the symbol. I find it difficult to express this in our terms without logical contradictions.

Thus the *Sharīʿa* came to be regarded as not something objectively distinct from the symbol "Islam," but inherent in it as its community aspect, so to speak. Since generations of Muslims strove to make the community-in-being conform to the image of Islam-as-community, they were compelled to spell out in precise detail the kinds of acts by which the two would be fused into a unity, and thus in a sense they objectivated the image. But what we criticize as the "theoretical" quality of the *Sharīʿa* is precisely the element in it that gave to it its symbolic value in Muslim thought. That both the spirit of the *Sharīʿa* and the kinds of acts that it prescribed might be widely and profoundly disregarded among Muslims was not overlooked, but was in no way felt to impugn the "*is*ness," the "reality" of the *Sharīʿa*.

This kind of symbolism is not limited to the religious sphere, however. It runs through all aspects and regions of Arab life and perhaps it will help to make the idea clearer if I mention some other examples. Take the Arabic script—itself a notation of symbols that recall a root structure out of which the reader has to extract for himself the objective, i.e., contextually relevant sense. The linguistic structure that it symbolizes, the classical Arabic, the *lugha*, is tenaciously and insistently maintained in spite of all purely rational, utilitarian, or technological arguments, and in spite of the fact that not one Arab uses it in colloquial speech—not simply because it is the language of the Qur'an, but because it is the precious and irreplaceable symbol of all that Arabs have meant to themselves and to the world. (And this, incidentally, is why the most perfect command of a colloquial dialect by a foreigner is less appreciated than a few stumbling sentences in the *lugha*.) And even the "High Dam" is a symbol. Egyptians are well aware that it will not solve Egypt's economic problems; but it is a symbol of the new determination of Egyptians to control for themselves the economic organization and destinies of their country, and, therefore, it already effectively exists, before a single stone has been put in place.

6

The criterion of the symbol, then, is not the objective or "materialist" criterion of "How does it work here and now?" but "Does it convey the essence of the reality, *al-haqq*, that which exists and to which a rightly ordered world would conform?" But because it conveys much more than its external form or meaning, its characteristic action is of a different order from what we should expect as its material objectivation. It carries a kind of spiritual potency for those who participate in varying degrees in an understanding of its significance, and because of this it initiates them into a fraternity and unites them by a common bond. Only those can really read classical Arabic who can "read between the lines" and vibrate in unison with the vibrations mediated by its symbols.

So the life of the Arabs (and also, I think, of the Persians), even in the modern world, is surrounded by symbols of many and various kinds, which remain impenetrable to outsiders—which, indeed, outsiders who observe them and take them in their literal meaning or as they seem to be expressed in objective forms, may regard as outmoded, absurd, quaint, ridiculous, perhaps even harmful for a balanced intellectual life or practical objectives. And even when the Arab or Persian borrows from the West, the borrowing (except in very narrow professionalized circles) becomes effective in the community as a whole only when it is elevated by or into a symbol. "Nationalism" is just such a symbol. Few Arabs have ever been able to define it in objective terms, or in any terms that would be unanimously endorsed, except in its negative connotation of freedom from foreign interference. Like other symbols, it performs the same function of binding together those who are moved by its potency, its aura. And by so doing, it superimposes common aims and ideals upon the multitude of small closed and even opposed groupings of ordinary daily life (without, however, superseding them)—family, clan, artisanal, professional—and has the power of uniting them in common action at specific moments and for specific causes. This is why there is felt to be *no* contradiction in principle between "Arab Nationalism" and Egyptian or Iraqi or other local nationalisms; they are distinguishable only in relation to the specific events that call them into play.

"Nationalism," then, as a symbol, does what in other dimensions of Islamic history "Islam" aimed to do, and in large measure succeeded in doing at different times and under the stimulus of specific events—i.e., override all divisive factors for a time in an emotional surge to achieve some end in which it is *at that moment* objectivated. When the emotional mood subsides, the old habits and attitudes of the separate groups resume their control of daily life and thought. But since "nationalism" operates as an active force only under the stimulus of emotion—being rationalized only in the thinking of a small minority—two consequences follow. One consequence is that the abstract symbol must be given concrete embodiment in the person of a "leader" upon whom emotional feeling can be more continuously focussed. But not *any* "leader." We have seen many "leaders" in these years who have conspicuously failed to rouse or to maintain the emotional fervor of the masses. For—and this is the second consequence—no emotional fervor can be sustained in the Islamic, or any other nation, unless the "leader" appeals to the profound subliminal roots of popular feeling. In the Middle East, at least, the two most powerful of these are the collective self-image of the community and the legacy of Islamic attitudes. This is why Mustafa Kemal was the greatest and most successful of all modern "leaders" in the Islamic world, being for all Turks the supreme embodiment of the traditional ideal of Turkish courage, and at the same time the Muslim hero, the *Ghazi*, who had challenged the insolence of the infidels and confounded their schemes and politics; and this is why the revolutionary government in Egypt consciously encourages the popular image of Col. 'Abd al-Nasir as the "new Saladin."

7

So we are brought back to Islam, and in the light of this long introduction we may, I hope, begin to see what it is in Islam that corresponds to secularism in Western thought. It is, in simple (perhaps too simple) terms, the rejection of the symbol in which all phenomena, whether of the external universe or of human life, find their ground of unity. Since in Muslim thought there is no other nexus of necessary causes, the rejection of this symbol resolves all unity and order into a jumble of chaotic fragments. This is, both intellectually and psychologically, a fearful price to pay—too high, far too high, a price for any but a tiny and unrepresentative minority.

Leaving aside for the present those whom we might call "out-and-out" secularists, it is a patent fact that large and increasing sectors of public life in the Muslim world appear to be dominated by the attitudes called "materialist," as the pervasive influences of Western thought and Western techniques strike root, more or less deeply, among intellectuals, middle classes, artisans, perhaps even in the villages, and the traditional rituals and rhythms of Muslim life weaken into disuse at an increasing rate. For these new components of life and thought must out, must find expression in some direction or other. But even if we limit our view to the so-called "intellectuals," those in whom the longest and deepest exposure to Western thought may be expected to have produced the most profound effects, it would be an error to regard them as pure rationalists, in any Western sense. For they are also the commissioned ranks and the missionaries of nationalism, and they cannot but be themselves emotionally involved with the great problem of all emergent nationalisms: "How can my nation, after centuries of decay and servitude, again 'become itself' and play its own distinctive and worthy part in the modern world?" The symbol of "nationalism" thus takes for them somewhat more concrete form in the "nation."

But the "nation" is not something to be made—it is there, with all its heritage of history, of symbolisms, of emotional ties and attitudes. If it is to be re-made, to "become itself," it must be re-made in a way which will preserve those things which characterize it as a nation.

8

So in each Muslim nation there can be seen in operation a parallel process, at different stages, and not always consciously pursued, as the effects of two or three generations of transplanted or engrafted Western thought begin to make themselves felt. What these have led to in the realm of ideas is not the denial of the traditional symbols, but the effort to redefine them in relation to various objective or existential events in the space-time continuum of terrestrial life. This is the real "Westernization" and the real meaning of that long and painful conflict, still unresolved, between *al-qadim* and *al-jadid*, the "old" and the "new," often misunderstood by Western observers as a conflict between the archaic and decaying forces of the Islamic tradition and the new broom of Western rationalism (or even of American pragmatism). I borrow from Jacques Bergue what seem to me to be the more realistic terms of the conflict, one between the "organic" and the "criticism."[1] It is, as I have just said, questionable whether the criticism—in any profound sense, as distinguished from superficial appearances—represents an *outright* rejection of the Tradition, since this would involve also the rejection of a great part of the national heritage and self-image. The object of the critics is not to discard the symbols, but rather to dissociate the symbols from past errors or outmoded methods of interpretation, and to cleanse them from the perversions and deformations by which, in the name of Tradition, they were exploited and degraded. They point to such perversions in the political and economic spheres, in the interests of autocratic and cynical governments and their hangers-on; in social institutions, by the

abuse of polygamy and divorce; and in the sphere of religious
life and institutions, by shutting the door on the use of reason
to re-examine its formulations, while opening it wide to dubious
"saints" and dervish charlatans, imposing on the credulity of
the masses.

But this is only a first step. The negative criticism by itself,
as the critics are well aware, would leave the social organism
disorganized and helpless in face of new problems. *Tajdīd*
implies "reconstruction," and the more difficult task which confronts the critics is to relate the symbols to new meanings, and
to new meanings of such inherent and immediate validity that
they can serve to give society, political, economic and social, a
new organic cohesion—no longer in medieval terms but in
terms that fit the conditions of the modern world. Such reconstruction in its early, blind, piecemeal stages has inevitably followed haltingly in the steps of the Western societies, but the
reformers remain convinced that "reconstruction" does not mean
the wholesale adoption of Western structures. To do so would
imply that the Islamic peoples, instead of "becoming themselves,"
would sink their individuality into the mass proletariat of the
West. What they seek to achieve is the reintegration in some
sense of what are felt to be Muslim-Arab, Muslim-Persian,
Muslim-Turkish, Muslim-Pakistani values and forces and to
give expression to them in modern and positive terms.

In *some* sense—but *what* sense, and how? This is the
agonizing question, this is the source of that psychological unset-
tlement and anxiety which, for anyone who reads modern Arabic
literature with careful attention, is its dominating note. It is
not surprising that some, weary of the inner conflict and ambigu-
ity, impatient at the slow processes of history, and in revolt
against the tenacious conservatism of the religious leaders, opt
for the clear-cut solution, the revolutionary rejection of the
Tradition, lock, stock, and barrel, and like the French Jacobins
would set up the Goddess of Reason as the only object of worship. These out-and-out or declared secularists may not be

numerous in a head count, nor very articulate. But there are
many times more who seem in practice to excise the explicitly
hyphenated Muslim part of their national heritage, to live (as
we should say) completely secularized lives in an atmosphere of
secular pursuits—not indeed worshiping the Goddess of Reason
in any rational manner, but floating with the current, openly
content to take things as they come and leave the solution of
these problems to the egg-heads and the future.

9

If this were all, then "Islam in the Modern World" would
have no meaning either for the present or the future. But this is
not all. Ask any one of the holiday-makers on the beaches of
Alexandria if he is a Muslim, and you will probably be taken
aback by the violence of his answer. "Islam" as a symbol retains
its emotional power. The inner grievance of the "critics" is that,
instead of playing its proper part in strengthening the national
morale and will and in overriding the selfish divisions of classes
or regional or other interested groups, it has been made to
appear an element of weakness and of division. This is the basis
of the resentment felt by some, the disinterest expressed by
others, at the conservatism of the 'ulama. The "renovators" (or
"innovators," according to the point of view) seem to be dis-
playing a curious, yet typical, reversion to the characteristic social
focus of religious activity in Islam. Negatively, they seek to
clear away the débris of the centuries from the pure mystery of
the symbol: "God's in His Heaven"—this is enough, we neither
need nor should ask to know more. The point of attack is the
image of His community in the world. Where the classical
jurists of Islam deduced this image from above, so to speak, the
"renovators" seek to objectivate it, in the modern manner, from
below. Where the "innovators" in the Christian world aim at
demythologizing its traditional theology, in the Muslim world

they aim at deconsecrating its traditional body of "revealed" law
—a significant indication, to repeat, of their continued involve-
ment in the triangular categories of Islam. In striving to recon-
struct the social angle—which naturally involves a complemen-
tary reconstruction of the historical angle as well—they discover,
as Dr. Sharabi indicates in his paper, a kind of moral personality
in participation in the struggle to realize their political and social
aspirations. But, in attaching objective values to political and
social institutions, they are operating under symbols that they
have so far failed to relate adequately to the Islamic ideology;
and, because of this, their symbols lack the emotional force, the
vibrations which alone can give them dynamic power within the
wider community, even if they may (and often do) exercise a
similar force within the coterie.

10

Finally, you may ask whether these aspirations and ideals
will eventually lead to a solution of the problems of Islam in
the modern world. Some Muslim theorists, for half a century
now, have dreamed of organized ecumenical councils to discuss,
decide on, and promulgate rulings on disputed points or new
demands. This kind of extrovert solution, I must confess, seems
to me an entirely illusory borrowing from Western ecclesiastical
history. Official Islam has always been the weakest point in
Islamic religious history, and the inner structure of Muslim
religious life would have to change radically before the con-
ciliar method could take root in it.

The traditional method of Muslim activism and renovation
has been the small "cell," the half-secret groups of consecrated
men and women who after long spiritual preparation issue into
the world with a message which, drawing its strength from the
symbol, spreads through widening circles the conviction of its
essential and existential rightness, its conformity with that "which

truly *is*." It is true that this method has led in the past and may well lead in the future to many false starts. But even false starts demonstrate the continuing vigor of the inner forces within Islam. And so long as these remain true to their ultimate symbols, somewhere along the line there will emerge the anonymous *mujaddid*, the "renovator," who will gather up all these ferments of the modern complex, set them in their true relationships, reformulate the triangle, and reintegrate the spiritual life and wholeness of the community.

But whether this, too, is a dream is for the future to show. For the present, the index of the vitality of Islam in a confusing and disordered world is precisely the sense of perplexity and distress that pervades an Islamic community which finds its familiar organisms no longer adequate but refuses to yield its conviction that God reigns.

---

1. Jacques Bergue, *Les Arabes d'Hier à Demain* (Paris, 1960), p. 14.

A Decade of Revolution: Social and Political Changes, 1949-1959

by

George F. Hourani

George F. Hourani is Associate Professor of
Arabic Studies at the University of Michigan.

A revolution is a sequence of comparatively rapid changes in the history of an area or a country, sometimes accompanied by violence as in the French and Russian revolutions, sometimes peaceful as in the industrial revolutions; but in all cases a certain break with the past is involved. In order to estimate just how revolutionary were these changes in the Arab countries, and in what respects, they should be set in the perspective of the whole history of the area.

The modern age in the Middle East began in the late eighteenth century, when the military impact of France and Russia forced the Turkish sultans on the path of military reform. Muhammad Ali in Egypt made the earliest moves toward industrialization and modern education during the first half of the nineteenth century, but accomplished little of permanent value owing to haphazard planning and vain military adventures. Of greater significance were the advances made after the middle of the century in Egypt and in other parts of the Ottoman empire. Between that time and World War I these areas acquired some railroads, telegraph and postal services, the first effective storage dams, governments organized on modern lines, and—most important of all—a few modern schools established by French, American and other educators, both missionary and secular. The fundamental nature of much of the work done in that period can be illustrated by the achievement of a British engineer, Sir William Willcocks, in Ottoman Iraq in the early years of the present century. His irrigation surveys and plans for the control and use of the Euphrates and Tigris remained the basis for projects harnessing those rivers until just a few years ago.[1] Internal progress, however, was accompanied by growing foreign domination of most of the Arab lands, so that prior to World War I the Middle East was still not considered a part of the modern world.

During the period between the two world wars more rapid advance was made in the fields of political, economic, social and educational development. I shall mention three of particular importance. One was the growth of nationalist movements into powerful forces, which were able to reverse the tide of imperialism and take long strides toward national independence. Another was the growth of a strong Jewish community in Palestine with Zionist aims, and the beginning of the struggle for the possession of that land. A third was the spread of modern industry in the area, led by the companies founded in Egypt by the Misr Bank.[2]

World War II had profound effects upon the Middle East. At its ending there was a good deal of independence, especially in internal affairs in several Arab states. The idea of Arab unity as a buttress for independence was in the air, and was embodied in a rudimentary fashion in the Arab League. But the British military forces and financial and commercial ties still remained important factors in Egypt, Iraq and Jordan. Even though these armed forces were discreetly kept at bases far from the big cities and after 1942 have not interfered in the internal affairs of these countries, the Arabs, as long as they were present at all, did not feel that their independence had really started. At the same time the Arabs had to face a startling new fact with which they were not ready to cope: the birth and growth of the state of Israel.

It should also be noted that, by mid-century, most Arab countries of the Middle East had governments organized on Western lines, with cabinets and parliaments, ministries and civil services. These governments were often inefficient and at times corrupt, but they at least provided a framework of order. Ideals of sound government were widely known and indeed practiced by many politicians and officials who nowadays receive little credit, owing to the general disrepute into which the regimes they served have fallen.

Some of the bigger cities were already nuclei of modern life, having many facilities for comfort and enjoyment, communication and education. In Cairo, Alexandria and Beirut, in particular, there were fair numbers of people who might be considered an urban elite. Industry was growing steadily in Egypt, Lebanon and Syria, while the more eastern countries had suddenly come upon vast fortunes through their mounting oil production, which was being developed by Western capital and skill. But rural development was slower, and land reform was an old problem that every politician was either unwilling or afraid to handle.

Altogether, then, we can say that, at the end of the 1940's, the Arab peoples had already made considerable progress toward the kind of life they desired. But some of the most necessary and most difficult steps had still to be taken in an environment of increasing complexity. These were the completion of independence, a satisfactory settlement of the Palestine problem, an effective degree of Arab unity, more honest and efficient government, further industrialization and urbanization, much greater rural development, land reform, and extension of education.

Against this background, I shall now survey the most important developments of the last ten years or so, beginning with some political matters.

1. *Independence.* With the withdrawal of the last French troops in 1946, the independence of Syria and Lebanon was completed. The British air bases in Iraq were handed over to Iraqi command in 1955. In 1956, Egypt came to the end of a long process of shaking off the British presence, and Sudan became an independent country in the same year. Jordan dis-

missed her last British officers in 1957. Thus, within a decade, six Arab states had gained independence.*

How did these countries gain their independence?

During World War II the Free French government had promised independence to Lebanon and Syria, and in 1945 was willing to grant it under certain conditions of alliance. Thus the two countries could have had limited independence by accepting those conditions. The fact that they won it without conditions was due to their own determination and ability to grasp opportunities, the French tactical blunders of bombarding Damascus and arresting a Lebanese cabinet in Beirut, and British governmental support of Syria and Lebanon at a time when superior British forces were still in those countries. This last was perhaps the decisive factor.

Iraq obtained the departure of the British Royal Air Force by accepting the Baghdad Pact. The Arabs, however, did not consider Iraq free until she had severed her alliance with Britain and the other Baghdad powers. This was accomplished by the revolution in 1958. In the first days of the revolution, the British government may have had serious intentions of backing an invasion from Jordan to restore the monarchy under King Husayn, but, as there was not the support for such a move from inside Iraq, it wisely refrained from action.

In the case of Egypt, two events merit consideration. The first was the Anglo-Egyptian Treaty of 1954, by which Britain agreed to evacuate her military base in the Canal Zone. The American Ambassador, Mr. Jefferson Caffrey, was prodding both parties to reach such an agreement, but we do not know how weighty was this influence. The most effective factors which resulted in the treaty seem to have been on the Egyptian side the firmness and businesslike attitude of the military government, on the British side respect for the new Egyptian government

---

* Saudi Arabia and Yemen were already free countries. The Aden protectorate and other coastal regions of Arabia continued under British control or advice in one form or another.

combined with an estimate that the base was no longer worth the cost of maintaining it in the face of Egyptian opposition. Another reason, given by Mr. Winston Churchill at the time, was that a small land base was no longer defensible under the conditions of nuclear warfare. It appears to me doubtful, however, that this was a valid reason, since Britain has not found it wise to abandon such other small strongholds as Gibraltar, Malta or Singapore, nor has any other great power abandoned its military bases or airfields. The withdrawal of Britain from the Canal Zone has still another puzzling aspect. She was surrendering her major base in the Middle East, yet she failed to follow it through with that major change in her foreign policy which seems to be implied, namely, the abandonment of her strategic interest in the area. The explanation perhaps lies in the confident expectation of the Conservative government of the time that the new treaty would safeguard British interests by its provisions for the return of British forces under certain circumstances. This assumption, however, makes the attack of 1956 appear all the more reckless, since it gambled with the treaty on which the whole remaining British position in the Middle East depended. The gamble failed and the treaty was destroyed.

The second event was the Anglo-French evacuation of Egypt at the end of 1956. The chief cause of this, as is well known, was international pressure. Perhaps it is worth noting that the most effective pressure came from an ally, the United States, just as in the evacuation of Syria and Lebanon pressure on France came from an ally, Great Britain.

Sudanese independence was rather easily gained. After Egypt and Britain agreed in 1953 that the Sudanese should make a free choice between independence or union with Egypt, the last serious obstacle to British withdrawal from Sudan was removed. The few resident British civil servants and army officers left without pressure on one side or regrets on the other. Britain had no desire to remain in a territory lacking strategic importance, and to go through the stale show of strikes and demonstrations which eventually would have led to the same end—independence.

Jordan's dismissal of the British officers and termination of the British alliance need little discussion. The government of Jordan was asserting its adulthood like a young man, and it had the right to do so. Britain, in turn, had no major interest in Jordan, and consequently did not oppose. It can be questioned, however, whether the break with Britain was in the interest of the Arab defenses along the Israel border.

Reviewing these rather easy victories, we see that in some cases the occupying power was pressed to withdraw by a stronger ally, and in others that it withdrew without pressure as the final step in an already completed evolutionary development. These latter cases can only be explained in the light of the history of the long struggle between Britain and the countries she ruled. The British became "fed up." This was due partly to their own idealism, which gave to so many Englishmen a distaste for unending interference with other nations' destinies, and partly to the persistence of the Arab national movements, which showed the unmistakable will of the Arabs for complete self-government. This persistence is shown nowhere more strikingly than in the history of modern Egypt. The Egyptians had no armed forces worth speaking of, no rugged or inaccessible territory, no important economic market like the Indians, no moral leadership to compare with Gandhi's. How did they do it? One is tempted to say, at first, by a clever use of opportunities. But that is not the real answer. The Egyptians simply wore out the British with their repeated demands of independence for over half a century.

There was yet another important factor, which favored national independence in the 1950's: the climate of world opinion. This was something intangible, but its effect was clear enough on the French withdrawal from Syria and Lebanon, and on the Anglo-French evacuation of Egypt in 1956. The United Nations on both occasions served as the focus of world opinion, and exercised effective influence when that opinion was substantially united.

What does the history of the last ten years indicate with regard to the durability of Arab independence? It indicates, in the first place, that there is something precarious about that independence, because the Arab countries were and are militarily defenseless against any major power. Throughout its history, the Arab Middle East has generally been governed by the strongest power within range and with an interest in it. Until 1918, it was ruled by the Ottoman Empire and Britain, from 1918 to the end of World War II by France and Britain. Now two other great powers are within range and display interest in the Middle East: the Soviet Union and the United States. Looking at the area in this larger perspective, do we have reason to hope that it will continue to enjoy its present measure of independence? Have world conditions and opinions changed so much that history will not be repeated? Certain signs of the times seem to indicate the contrary.

We must start with the fact that Russia has for long shown strategic interest in this region, and would still like to control it. But it is also evident that she is not prepared to risk a world conflict for the possession of the Middle East. This has become clear in the successive crises of Azerbaijan, Iranian oil, American bases in Turkey, the Suez attack and the Iraq revolution. The Western powers, on the other hand, had shown a disposition to intervene in the area in order to prevent the loss of vital advantages. After the fiasco of the Anglo-French attack on Egypt in 1956, the United States assumed the responsibility for the preservation of these advantages and has evidently concluded that Arab neutrality would not injure them seriously. But whenever there appeared a danger of two things, instability in the area or the threat of Communist control in any part of it, the United States did not hesitate to act. This was illustrated in 1956 by the readiness of the Sixth Fleet in the Eastern Mediterranean to prevent, on the one hand, Soviet military aid to Egypt, on the other, the extension of the conflict by England and France. On a smaller scale the swift landing of Marines in Lebanon in the summer of

1958 helped to settle a situation that could have led to strife in the whole area and might easily have turned to the advantage of Soviet Communism. This landing was historic because it was the first armed intervention of the United States in the Middle East. The early departure of the Marines was also significant, as it proved the intent of this country to intervene as little as possible. This was also demonstrated by the restraint exercised by the United States during the past two years in watching the dangerous rise of Communism in Iraq without attempting to arrest it—a calculated risk which is now apparently paying off.

Having stressed so far the precariousness of Arab independence, I wish to point out also some elements of strength which it has. There is a new consciousness of national identity which pervades the whole Arab world. The Arabs are now politically more alert. Today it would not be easy for any foreign power to maintain control over the Arab countries. It is one thing to send military forces into the area at the invitation of a government, but quite another matter to try to rule it.

All these factors are likely to carry more weight with non-Communist powers, and that is one good reason why the Arab countries should align themselves with the West if they find they cannot safely maintain their present neutrality.

2. *The Conflict with Israel.* The establishment of the state of Israel in 1948 exerted decisive influence upon the foreign relations of the Arab states, for it meant that they now had a non-Arab state in their midst, which they neither desired nor accepted. At once, the Arabs adopted a policy of hostility toward the "intruder," only to realize with a shock their inability to dislodge the new state or prevent its consolidation. This realization of impotence has been at once the greatest blow to Arab pride and the greatest stimulus to effort. It has caused the overthrow of incompetent governments;[3] it has brought about the economic boycott of Israel as a measure short of war; and, most important of all, it has stimulated the drive for Arab unity as a political and economic necessity.

Since the debacle of 1948-49, almost nothing has changed outwardly in the relationship of the Arabs with Israel. The boundaries remain frozen on the lines where the fighting stopped, running through the center of Jerusalem and separating villages from their farmlands. The Arab refugees are still in their depressing refugee camps and refuse to return to their old homes or move to new ones. Official relations between the two sides are still those of an armistice, with nonrecognition and no trade or travel between them. The feelings of Arabs and Israelis toward each other remain the same to all appearances. A solution to their quarrel is not in sight. But is it possible to believe that nothing has changed in human minds and hearts over a period of more than ten years? I believe that in many unacknowledged ways the two parties are more disposed to reach a settlement than they were at the beginning.

3. *Unity*. The League of Arab States has provided an organization through which the various states can work together by voluntary cooperation in all spheres. It has been effective in cultural measures, such as the standardization of school curricula, and in economic measures, such as the Arab Development Bank. In politics it has sometimes served as the representative organ of the Arab states, but it is in this sphere that its limitations became most apparent. Like the Confederation which preceded the United States of America, the Arab League has been able to act politically only within the limits of unanimous consent of all the states, and this rule has proved ineffective in times of crisis. The Arab-Israeli war has clearly shown that the League was unable to produce the unified military action which was necessary for success in the war. This failure, more than anything else, led in the 1950's to deeper thinking on unity among the Arabs, and gave a stronger impulse to political unification through federation.

The pace of achievement in this second stage of Arab unity has been slow. Nevertheless, we have witnessed two closely related developments of great significance in the past few years. One was the general recognition of Nasir of Egypt as leader of Arab unity.[4] The other development was the union of Egypt and Syria into the United Arab Republic in 1958, the first union between two Arab states.

The opportunity for a Pan-Arab Nasirite movement was presented by the governments of Great Britain and France in 1956. By his successful defiance of these two great powers, Nasir became a political hero of the Arab world. Nasirism, as a form of Pan-Arabism, reached its peak in 1958 with the establishment of the United Arab Republic, the ferment in Lebanon and the overthrow of the monarchy in Iraq.

Since then Nasirism has been held in check by the governments of the Arab countries surrounding Egypt and Syria, and we do not know at present whether this movement was merely a faltering step which will proceed no further or the first step leading to a wider union. The obvious reason for the recent check of Nasirism may be found in the concern of the other Arab governments for their own survival and in the methods of persuasion used by the "Voice of the Arabs," by the Egyptian press and other media of propaganda. They have been somewhat indelicate in their heavy attacks on the governments of neighboring Arab countries, and this has stimulated reactions of local patriotism. Thus, the governments of Iraq, Jordan, Saudi Arabia and Sudan have been able to draw upon a certain amount of public backing for their refusal to be rushed into union. The one successful union so far, that of Egypt and Syria, came about through the request of the government of the smaller country, Syria, and was voluntary on both sides. It seems, therefore, that Arab political unity cannot be forced through the leadership of one man, however able and devoted he may be, but has to be accepted by every Arab state. Much will depend on how attractive the United Arab Republic is going to appear to the rest of the Arab Middle East in the next decade. This, in turn, depends on many things, such as the prosperity and progress of Egypt and Syria, the extent of Syrian participation in the Federal government of the United Arab Republic, and the respect shown by the "Voice of the Arabs" for the governments of other Arab countries.

4. *Revolutionary governments.* During the 1950's, revolutionary governments were established in Egypt, Syria, Iraq and Sudan. If we are to generalize about the way such governments arise, perhaps all we can say is that they do so in countries with a great deal of discontent and little experience in political democracy. To understand the reasons for discontent in these four Arab countries we should mention the following:

In all of them there were parliamentary governments, with or without a monarchy. Parties used to compete at elections, cabinets were appointed, dismissed or reshuffled, but the frequent political changes had no effect on the real problem that needed solution. The party platforms hardly varied from each other, as they all were in favor of social justice, Arab unity and prosperity without being too specific about the ways by which these aims were to be realized. Besides, the parties were often hardly more than organizations to support the political careers of small groups of individuals.

The main problems, such as Palestine, ignorance and poverty remained unresolved. But these problems could be dealt with only by more efficient governments, and the existing regimes were unable to produce governments to satisfy an impatient public. Why was the public impatient? One reason was the defeat in Palestine, which the public felt was a national disgrace. (It may not have been accidental that military revolutions happened first in Syria and Egypt, which were more closely involved in Palestine than in Iraq and Sudan.) Another reason for public impatience sprung from the very fact of independence. It had been the custom formerly to blame the foreign occupying powers for all troubles. Now that the welfare of the people was in the hands of Arab leaders, it was expected that they would act to improve conditions and solve the basic problems.

Why did the revolutions take a military form? Civilians could act only through the parliamentary parties and were bound to get involved in all the compromises and hesitations that went with the parliamentary system. Military officers, on the other hand, held advantages for action that the civilians lacked. They had physical power, and training that qualified them to use it. They were not held back by the traditions of civilian rule; they could suspend parliamentary governments, and thus break through the vicious cycle of regimes that were unable to reform themselves. Military officers, moreover, were closer to the common people, since they generally sprung from the lower-middle classes and not from aristocratic families, and reflected in their actions the hopes of the people.

Nasir of Egypt is perhaps the best illustration of what has just been said. His outstanding qualities are his great zeal and strong will. These qualities are fortunately combined with a sincere dedication to the well-being of his country and the cool intelligence of a chessplayer or military instructor. By dissolving the popular forces of the Wafd, the Muslim Brotherhood, and replacing General Naguib, Nasir showed skill in timing and a realistic use of key forces in the army and the trade unions.[5] After he had aroused an international storm over the Suez Canal in 1956, he behaved like a good yachtsman who knows how far he can sail into the wind and when he must run with it.

Nasir's limitations reflect the shortcomings of his education and experience. His power of expression is not above average. He lacks the finesse of the upper-class Egyptian. He had no opportunity to travel outside of the Arab world prior to 1955. Since then he has visited Yugoslavia, Indonesia, India and the Soviet Union, but he has not yet visited a Western country.* (The only known invitation he received from the West was in August, 1956, to the first London conference on the Suez Canal, but this was more like a summons, which he was bound to refuse under the circumstances.)

Of course, Nasir does not rule the United Arab Republic

---

* Nasir attended the meeting of the Assembly of the United Nations in the fall of 1960.

alone. He depends on his ministers for information and advice. But it should be remembered that his closest associates are men of his own background, that Nasir has always been the leader among them, and that he was the man who made the big decisions—so that more depends on what he learns and accepts, than on the advice he receives. His ability and willingness to profit from experience will therefore mean very much for the future of the United Arab Republic and the Arab World.

*   *   *

With regard to the social revolution of the 1950's, the extensive and fundamental efforts at social improvement merit particular attention.

Observers of the Middle East until recent times have always emphasized the sharp division of the Arab population into two main classes, a small wealthy landed class which governed, and a mass of peasants who existed to serve and supply their landlords. The outstanding fact of the past decade has been the greatly reduced sharpness of this division. This is particularly true in Egypt, Syria and Iraq, where the political revolutions produced a new class structure.[6]

The wealthy landed class has lost most of its former importance. Instead, a new and rapidly growing urban middle class has taken over the leadership in all areas of political, economic and cultural activity. The peasants, freed from their former servitude, are beginning to experience the benefits of greater economic independence.

The present influence and power of the middle class springs partly from their position in government, industry and commerce, and partly from their broader education. The army officers, who led the political revolutions to success in the 1950's, belong to the middle class. The administrative and technical personnel of the government, now in charge of the development and establishment of social improvements, are members of the middle class. So are the students of the universities and institutions of higher learning who will be the future leaders.[7]

Perhaps the most important social improvement undertaken in the Middle East during the last ten years was land reform, which has completely changed the status of the peasant masses. Egypt was the first country to reduce the size of estates held by one family to a maximum of 300 acres. It took courage and determination to proceed against a class which owned most of the land and which, for centuries, had dominated the government. Naṣir and his officers possessed such determination because they were convinced of the support of the middle class and the peasant majority for a much needed land distribution. That they were confronted with practical difficulties due to the new owners' lack of experience and capital, and the small size of the new peasant estates, is natural. But institutions for agricultural credit, cooperation and education were developed by the state to meet these problems. The present Egyptian government has successfully forestalled the spread of Communism by this reform in a country that was otherwise fair game for collectivization.

The same development is taking place in Syria, the northern province of the United Arab Republic. In Iraq, too, the revolutionary government is carrying out a genuine land reform which should help to outwit the Communists. It is a platitude of politics that landowning farmers are the strongest opponents of collectivized farming.

In Lebanon, Jordan and Yemen, maldistribution of land is not such an acute problem, and consequently it has received less attention. In Saudi Arabia, tribal ownership and grazing rights produce entirely different land problems.

Besides land reform, rural welfare also received the attention of the governments. So far Egypt has carried out the most substantial projects for the improvement of village life. Village social centers for health, welfare, adult education and recreation were already begun in the last years of the monarchy by the imaginative Minister of Social Affairs, Ahmad Husayn. These have been reorganized under the Republic as "Combined Centers," and are being increased in number to have them within reach of the whole rural population.[8]

Among the social improvements, special reference should be made to the great efforts of the Arab governments in the field of education. The present target of all ministries of education is universal and compulsory primary education in the rural areas as well. During the last decade, very substantial progress has been made in this respect, and school attendance has more than doubled. It is hoped that, within the next decade or two, illiteracy will be greatly reduced if not eliminated.[9]

In the cities, special attention has been paid to the establishment and development of vocational technical schools, teacher training schools, colleges and universities. In 1949, there were state universities in Cairo, Alexandria and Damascus, foreign universities in Cairo and Beirut (two), and the noted Azhar for Islamic studies in Cairo. Most of these were enlarged and improved in the 1950's, and several new ones have been added, such as the universities of 'Ayn Shams, Asyut, Khartum, Baghdad, the Lebanese University in Beirut, and the Hikma University in Baghdad which is a Catholic institution. As more and more students with better secondary education enter universities, standards of education are steadily rising, and with them a better understanding of the problems which need solutions, as well as a greater eagerness to participate in their solution.[10]

* * *

Having briefly surveyed some of the fundamental political and social changes that have taken place in the Middle East during the last decade, some mention should also be made of the unsolved problems which will require attention in the next decade.

1. The independence of all coastal areas of the Arabian peninsula will certainly be a target of the Arabs. Without the independence of these areas, the independence of the Arab lands cannot be considered complete. Certainly, the capacity of the Arabs of Aden, Hadramawt and the Persian Gulf to govern themselves or participate in the government of neighboring Arab states can no longer be questioned. If the directors of British

colonial policy in these regions are as alert as they have been in other parts of Africa, they will forestall conflict by a graceful retirement, as in the Sudan.

2. Eventually the conflict with Israel will have to be resolved, but another decade may have to go by before the necessary spirit of conciliation and concession will appear on both sides. Meanwhile, it will be one of the tasks of statesmanship on both sides to prevent a repetition of 1956.

3. Another major task for the statesmen of the 1960's will be the achievement of political unity. Great benefits would surely accrue to the Arabs from a union of all Arab states. Therefore, present and future governments cannot sidestep this important problem.

4. Every government, even the best, needs public criticism and the participation of its citizenry in the country's affairs. Egypt, therefore, with a tradition of parliamentary government and free debate prior to 1952, and with a rapidly growing educated public will have to return to a parliamentary system, introduce truly democratic elections and establish a free press.

In due course of time Syria and Iraq will follow Egypt's example, while in Lebanon, with the problem of sectarian division of its population, constitutional reform is needed for the proper functioning of democracy.

The states of the Arabian peninsula and the Sudan must first introduce reforms and expand public education before democratic governments can be established.

5. The social and economic reforms already achieved in the more advanced Arab countries should be extended over the whole of the Arabian peninsula. This task offers vast opportunities of pioneering for Arabs with education and skill.

6. Higher education and original research in all Arab countries are in need of substantial improvement. Whether it is due to government control, too heavy teaching loads or too low salaries, the faculties of Arab universities have not yet achieved that degree of distinction in creative thought which would make

foreigners eager to work among them or to learn Arabic, as was the case in the Middle Ages. But originality takes time to blossom, and we should not be impatient. Those of us who know the cultural history and intellectual vitality of the Arab people have no doubt that they will once more contribute things of value to the total human heritage.

1. S. Longrigg, *Iraq, 1900 to 1950* (New York, 1953), pp. 63, 371 ff.
2. C. P. Issawi, *Egypt at Mid-Century* (New York, 1954), pp. 156, 225-227.
3. See Gamal Abdul Nasir, *The Philosophy of the Revolution* (Cairo, no date), pp. 10-15.
4. Ibid., pp. 55, 65, 72.
5. See especially J. and S. Lacouture, *L'Egypte en mouvement* (Paris, 1956).
6. H. A. R. Gibb and H. Bowen, *Islamic Society and the West* (New York, 1950), I, Part 1, p. 280.
7. *The Arab World*, IV, (1958), Nos. 2-5.
8. N. Barbour, "Impressions of the United Arab Republic," *International Affairs*, XXXVI, (1960), p. 25.
9. *International Year Book of Education*, XX, (1958), pp. 183-190.
10. *International Year Book of Education*, XX, (1958), pp. 183-190.

Political and Intellectual Attitudes of the Young Arab Generation

by

Hisham Sharabi

Hisham Sharabi is Associate Professor of History and Government at Georgetown University.

A strict empirical approach to the political and intellectual attitudes of the younger Arab generation would attempt to classify and describe those attitudes scientifically. It would treat of such topics as Arab nationalism, Communism, neutralism, attitudes toward the West and Israel, and it would analyze Arab literature, listing specific problems which Arab intellectuals face or ignore. I do not intend to do this.

My starting point and the limit of my discussion converge upon the political and intellectual *crisis* in which the younger Arab generation finds itself today. Let me add immediately that this approach lays no claim to scientific demonstrability, nor does it pretend to preserve an attitude of strict ethical neutrality. If my observations therefore appear to be excessively critical or somewhat negative in tone, this is due partly to the fact that there seem to me insufficient grounds for optimism in the present situation, but mostly to the belief that it is better not to accept things at their face value even though one may prove to be in the long run mistaken.

Reduced to its simplest components, the crisis may be defined in terms of the opposition between efficacy as a principle of action and rationality as a principle of legal accommodation, between power as it becomes progressively more concentrated and personalized, and freedom as it gradually loses its political and institutional foundations. The crisis in this light has little to do with the *form* of government or, more precisely, with democracy as a formal principle of political organization. Charismatic leadership, as Max Weber pointed out, is temporary by definition, and the legitimacy of revolutionary power resides not in some vague principle of democracy but in another kind of principle that sets up loyalty to the original goals and the aspirations of revolution as its highest values.

The Arab revolution, like all other revolutions, asserts the ascendancy of hope over all forms of degradation and despair and reaffirms the capacity of men to achieve justice and freedom in the concrete reality of a social order. But such an order is born on the first day and with the first gesture of defiance, and its deliberate relegation to a later date in the name of transitional necessity inevitably ends with its distortion or total abandonment and thus with betrayal of the original goals and aspirations of the revolution. What will take root and last are not the ephemeral victories of the transitional period—the verdicts of the people's courts, the slogans of the street mobs, the speeches delivered from balconies and over the radio—but rather the guiding ideas embodied in laws and institutions, the values translated into habits of thinking and of doing, the attitudes of spirit marking the lasting triumphs of a conscious and self-directing society.

To study this crisis, it is first necessary to view it briefly from the standpoint of the contemporary Arab intellectual, then to analyze it in terms of the political challenge it offers the younger Arab generation as a whole.

Put directly, the intellectual crisis of the younger Arab generation may be summarized in terms of three main features: psychological uprootedness, loss of moral and religious certainties, and valuational drift.

To begin with, when we say "uprooted," we are not referring to the Levantine type of Arab who is found in all large cities and towns from Beirut to Tangiers and to whom cultural and psychological uprootedness is a normal state of being, but to the entire literate Arab generation that has come into manhood in the mid-twentieth century to find itself disinherited in a world providing no values or certainties that are not relative and contingent. The one force, Islam, which provided its fathers with at least the necessary assurance to render this world a familiar and habitable place, if not with the inspiration and strength to build a new society, appears to have ceased to carry any real meaning to the younger generation. The last and perhaps the only genuine movement of Islamic revival stemming from this generation was the Muslim Brotherhood; this group was destined to win or to lose everything, because it presented an absolute solution that permitted no compromise. Its destruction by the revolutionary movement in Egypt in 1954 marks the beginning of total secularism in contemporary Arab politics. Islam, it is true, still cushions the established pattern of life of the older generation and of the illiterate masses, but as a metaphysic it no longer exercises a genuine hold on the mind of youth. To young nationalists, Islam holds more meaning as part of the national heritage than as an all-embracing view of man and the world.

Sitting among the ruins of this shattered world, today's young Arab intellectual has so far refused to face the needs implicit in the rebuilding of his world. The vital task of defining and formulating the fundamental problems inherent in his condition, which he alone can properly perform, he has left to Christian and European scholars whose works are just about all the knowledge the Arab has of himself, of his present, and of his past. Self-knowledge achieved through the eyes of others remains at best external, limited and inadequate; so it is in the intellectual atmosphere of the contemporary Arab world, which lacks real subjectivity and the capacity for self-criticism on any profound level. It is not surprising, therefore, that beneath the thin exterior of the Arab intellectual's aggressive self-confidence there exists in reality a solitary void and a lostness that await the remedy provided only by the turning of the mind upon itself. In a way, this is a state of adolescence in which doubt and the simultaneous need to believe set a limit to consistent, logical thought and make the urge to dream and to talk an imperative psychological necessity. Meaning loses its measurable content, and appearance holds precedence.

But who is the Arab intellectual? He is, simply, the writer, the journalist, the teacher, the lawyer, the student, the government official and the educated Army officer. He is a separate individual in that the group to which he belongs on the intellectual level possesses on the social level no special status. Taken as an individual he is generally solemn and serious and wholly lacking in a sense of humor—though often not in wit. He is capable of great pedantry, not because of intellectual dishonesty but because of the need to live up to his position as a man who thinks for himself. Usually he is endowed with a natural grace of gesture and a verbosity which his rich and beautiful language makes almost imperative. He is allergic to precision and brevity. When he writes or speaks publicly, he is usually extravagant, addicted to superlatives. In private, he is eager, sentimental, and sincere. His mind, already impregnated with too much color and noise, cannot be impressed except by ever sharper contrasts. This is well illustrated by the predicament of modern Arabic literature: with the exception of some of the younger writers of Egypt during the thirties, some Iraqi writers of the immediate postwar period, and a few individual writers of contemporary Lebanon and Tunisia, modern Arabic literature has really very little to offer. It is too eloquent, too obvious, too direct; in it there is no "implication," no "turning away," no "silence." The writer does not allow his reader to enjoy insinuations or shades of meaning, to work out suggestions, or to interpret hidden intentions. Whatever the subject matter, the picture is always Raphaelian in size, exaggerated, and overpowering. What is conveyed and what is received seem always accompanied by loud music. The ear is perhaps delighted, but the intelligence is oppressed.

By eluding direct and responsible confrontation of the fundamental issues that face him, the Arab intellectual has succeeded in erecting almost insurmountable barriers between himself and the truly meaningful currents of his tradition. The apologist and the propagandist still dominate the intellectual stage, addressing an inattentive foreign audience in order to receive enthusiastic but uncritical applause at home. A few solitary rebels, like Muhammad Abdu, Abdul Raziq, and Taha Hussein, who attempted to turn their critical vision inward, were promptly suppressed and forced to compromise. They are the symbols of the mind's defeat in the Arab's modern awakening. Today, all that is living and vital in Arab heritage remains alien and remote. The Prophet Muhammad himself, symbol and central source of this heritage, who insisted upon his own common humanity, is not really viewed as a man to be loved and understood and communicated with, but as a vague, distant figure, shrouded in formal adulation and beyond reach; the great Mu'tazilites, those true Greeks of Islam, the Sufis, Ibn Rushd, Ibn Khaldun, all are outside the living consciousness of this disinherited mind. But al-Ghazzali is still with us, his victorious conciliation still setting the limits of reason's kingdom, still suppressing the mind's passion to dare. Symbolically (but also perhaps literally), it seems that without dethroning al-Ghazzali, the Arab mind cannot fully liberate itself. It will remain imprisoned in its present landscape, peopled not by the true heroes of the mind but by the leaders and villains of temporal politics. In this landscape there could be no provision for the permanent or the eternal; good and evil are reflected in its leaders and villains; a Manichaean ethic predominates.

Cut off from his heritage, the young Arab intellectual has to import his ideologies. In itself, the impact of the West is dizzying; even greater is the state of intellectual and moral suspension which this impact creates. To a mind hungering for certitudes, multiplicity of values does not contribute to an inner sense of direction; a culture which offers reason and method as normative principles of thought and action rather than philosophic finalities cannot be assimilated without distortion. From this vertiginous tension, there appears to be no easy escape. The solution offered by Kemalist Turkey seems no more satisfactory than that offered by Lebanon or Tunisia. It is now quite obvious that on any profound level Westernization through state legislation is as sterile in the long run as any partial compromise. There is no evading the fact that nothing can be imposed on the mind from the outside. In the final analysis, the mind has to recreate its own world in its own image.

It is true that history has been ruthless with the Arab intellectual of the contemporary generation: it entered his world by frontal attack, as it were. He had to face it unprepared, with his native intelligence and his capacity to endure as his only weapons. If he has been led astray by miscalculation, if he has accepted certain forms of falsehoods, if he has failed to recognize the obligations imposed upon him by his task, he cannot be justly accused of having succumbed. On the contrary, his solipsistic vision of history, his thinking in terms of a separate world exclusively his, and his stubborn pride have already begun to give way before the realization that dignity and freedom and happiness are longings common to all men and that in this world there always exists the hope for a higher destiny and a will for genuine fraternity among men. It is in this realization, now focused upon the plight of the rising masses in the Arab world, that the intellectual issue of the younger Arab generation is transformed into a political challenge.

For the sake of argument, I shall state my point here in a purposely formal and general way: since the beginning of history, the masses have been exploited and betrayed, against all humanitarian and religious injunctions, by the minority. Now in the Arab world at the turn of the mid-century, when the masses are for the first time awake and conscious, when genuine liberty as well as a better and more abundant life for all have become possible, the question presents itself: will the masses be again betrayed? This is the fundamental question that underlies the political challenge facing the younger Arab generation.

Wherever the revolution has triumphed, the ideal of building a new society has also triumphed. The concept of radical reform, of complete economic and social transformation—that is, the concept of the welfare state—has also brought with it the reality of total power. Today the state is supreme: it is the repository of all power as well as the guardian of all hope. Ironically, after ridding themselves of Europe's political control, the Arabs have now fallen victim to the most pernicious of Europe's dream, that born of the suffering and conflict of the last hundred and fifty years and of the incurable nostalgia of Western man from Plato to Marx—the dream of building on the ruins of an unacceptable and a repudiated present the ideal of the just and happy society of the future.

To what extent the present is willing to pay the sacrifice for the future in the brave new Arab world cannot yet be determined, but the new climate of hopeful and eager activism carries some prediction of the shape of things to come. Already, recourse to extreme means is being justified in terms of *rational* ends, and violence is being legitimized in terms of superior values. No doubt political exigencies may require giving precedence to certain pragmatic considerations over principles that may appear abstract in the light of these exigencies, but it is not the sense of political realism which is here at issue. In this, as in every similar historical situation, the fundamental point is that power cannot be curbed once it has become, and recognizes itself as, supreme. Indeed, facts in themselves have little meaning. On the level of political action, total subordination of moral principles to facts finally leads to political sterility. Cynical repression replaces inspired leadership, and sullen acquiescence enthusiastic backing. Not only the principle of political liberty is at stake here, but the entire movement of revolution and hope. I believe it is not going too far to say that once real communication between ruler and ruled breaks down, a deadlock follows from which there is no escape except by resorting to violence. The counterrevolution not only brings an end to the movement of revolution itself but, being the expression of disenchantment and therefore in some fashion reactionary, also repudiates that revolution's aspirations and goals.

Again, the sentimental idealism which motivates political

thought and action in the Arab world cannot long escape its inherent contradictions for, as Europe has so well taught us, all revolutions that lay claim to absolute good end by erecting the absolute state. The ideal of the welfare state, in other words, is never enough. The masses could be better fed only to be better enslaved. Palpable justice, like certainty, is above all an approximation in the concrete. And in the end, freedom and hunger are inextricably bound: to satisfy one at the expense of the other is to serve injustice equally. Nothing provides better food for tyranny than the promise of future freedom made in justification of temporary repression; one fears that the younger Arab generation is already learning how to tolerate its humiliations in the name of that promise. There is no escaping the pragmatic fact that the sovereignty of both individual conscience and social justice is shattered by a revolution that has lost its original sincerity and good faith. No wonder if in some countries the difference between political assassination and judicial murder is already fast disappearing!

To the Arab intellectual there is no avoiding the political. To divorce oneself from the political struggle represents not merely failure to perform one's duty, but, above all, forfeiture of a vital right that symbolizes one's personal integrity. The ironic fact is, however, that at precisely the moment when the revolution finally achieved its political goal in the Arab countries, the younger generation suddenly found itself barred from full and free participation in political life. In the centralized state which now came into being, real power became securely embodied in personal leadership, and the former voluntary and fraternal alliances between the various parties and groups within the nationalist movement were now replaced by the new leadership's demand for conformity and compliance. Yesterday's free and easy comradeship was transformed into a relationship of leader and led; now the multiplicity of views has to be sacrificed for unity symbolized by the single will.

It is this contradiction, which, more than any other single

factor, came to light with the political victory of the revolution
and is responsible for bringing about simultaneously the crystal-
lization of absolute personal leadership and the impoverishment
of political life. I am speaking here, not of the artificial multi-
party system of the former corrupt parliamentary governments
of Nuri as-Sa'id and Nahas Pasha, but of the failure of the new
revolutionary regimes to devise a system of government in which
both free and continuous communication between ruler and
ruled and the possibility of political organization and opposition
are preserved. Instead, what has happened and is in large part
responsible for the present situation is that the new leadership
has been able to prop itself upon the total, almost mystical support of the half-awakened masses without having to resort to the
intermediary agency of political parties and groups; legality no
longer needs the vote—it derives it directly from a mystic delega-
tion of power by the people. This is perhaps the reason the attitude of the new leadership in the Arab world toward any form
of political organization is expressed either by perfunctory assent
to restricted party activity, as in Iraq, or by contemptuous sub-
limation of energies through a single national organization shorn
of any real power, as in the United Arab Republic. One can
only observe here that, by consciously or unconsciously trans-
ferring military principles to social and economic life, the social
proletarianization of the Arab masses is being accelerated and,
on the political level, the precollectivist stage is being set.

We all know that in any plebiscite the new leadership can
easily win a sweeping national vote. But this in itself can never
be taken as sufficient protection against the hazards of sudden
and unexpected changes and the inevitable end of a charismatic
type of leadership. The danger constantly imminent is the dis-
ruption of the impalpable link which binds the leadership to the
masses and presently constitutes the sole basis of stability and
order. Once the masses lose their enthusiasm, once the mystical
unity is broken and groups begin to form, leadership is isolated
and has no choice but the irrevocable one of taking refuge in

the only means at its disposal—physical force. This is unavoidable; even under the best circumstances communication between leader and led is imperfect, inasmuch as it is always one-sided, because it excludes debate and is never fully reasoned. Thus the terror of isolated and solitary power hangs upon the political scene like a scepter. The only way out seems to be through adopting a system of mediation and of sharing responsibility which only full and free participation in political life can provide.

As we know, the only alternative to free and organized political activity is mob action. Driven into the street, one is left with only one effective medium of expression: demonstration. From the point of view of political dignity, this is the ultimate form of degradation. From it, there is no escape in the long run except in revolt and suicidal violence.

It cannot be overemphasized that, without spokesmen and without mediation, reasoned dialogue is impossible and propaganda becomes the sole means of communication. In the terrible silence that follows, the Arab intellectual finds himself driven either to compliance or to exile, to prostitution or to solitude. To those young intellectuals who are aware—that is, to those who strive for harmony between conduct and thought—exile no longer consists solely of being physically banished from their country; the most bitter kind of exile now assumes the form of domestic acquiescence, of putting the mind under arrest.

It is not, as I said earlier, a question of opposing the revolutionary movement; on the contrary, from the standpoint of the younger Arab generation, it is simply a question of not being allowed to play a role in the revolution, to serve it, to become part of it. To be called upon to serve the revolution by approving the silence it enforces—that is, to accept everything and to sacrifice everything until circumstances permit fulfillment of the original hopes and promises—is to be asked to accept a new principle of morality, a new ethic of expediency which will not only obstruct any true fulfillment of those hopes and promises but will also indefinitely subordinate such fulfillment to the blind will of circumstance. It is inevitable that those who choose compliance and accept the silence are forced by these very circumstances to cultivate the virtues required for success in these changed and changing times. It therefore should not be surprising if in the new hierarchy of wealth, rank and power—where conversation is dead and silence reigns despite the clamor of voices —servility and the bended knee become chief requisites not only for forging ahead but also for earning a mere living. As we all know, new virtues create new vices; for the Arab, the most abhorrent of the latter is dishonor.

It is as easy as it is comforting to indulge in self-pity, and for the Arab intellectual this seems to have become almost a passion. Since self-pity is really only one step removed from self-justification, the Arab intellectual tends to derive no little satisfaction in viewing himself as a victim. But victim he is not. To tell the truth, his generation has benefited most abundantly. After all, the mid-century has brought an end to the humiliation of being a man under foreign rule; it has provided the Arab of this generation adequate education, the opportunity for decent work, and the means for material well-being; above all, it has offered him the fruits of the older generation's struggle to attain national independence, dignity, and the chance to engage finally in the positive task of building a free and happy society. Leadership has not been lacking either. Nor can the revolution be doubted, whether in Egypt, in Iraq, in the Sudan, or in North Africa.

Perhaps this generation, or rather its intellectual vanguard, needs to heed Nietzsche's advice to rid itself before everything else of the poison of self-pity. One can then see better and perhaps also speak out, thus assuming the responsibility of taking a position. But responsibility, as a political act, is never really effectual except in solidarity; and solidarity can only be achieved in the cheerful and confident climate of rational debate and discussion, never in absolute unanimity. It is only in such a climate that this generation can best face up to the political challenge that confronts it and at the same time prepare itself to fulfill the task laid upon it.

This task first demands that the Arab intellectual render rational the meaning of the revolution so that it is consistent with and faithful to the ideals of freedom and justice in their concrete, everyday application. It is a task that requires of him the moral courage not to accept anything unreservedly except the freedom to speak out and his right to integrity as a man. Beyond this, no course of action can be defined.

To conclude, it seems always true that whenever one is called upon to act, one has to think, to choose, to decide, in terms of the specific situation, which is ever unique and unforeseeable. Although it is also true, as Goethe put it, that thought cripples and action narrows, the dichotomy here is nevertheless artificial; neither the plunge into blind activism nor withdrawal into disinterested thought can be accepted as exclusively valid. In doing as in thinking, all our striving is toward an approximation that renders existence a little more tolerable, a little more meaningful. Such things as gentleness and ease, moderation and tolerance, strength and generosity are both desirable and reachable. In this realm, false profundity is incapable of confusing the issue. The real is unmistakable, and concrete ends can be reconciled with just means. For in the end, there is nothing more practical or more effective than the cool hand of reason; action can indeed know its meaning and recognize the limit of its efficacy.

On the intellectual level, the younger Arab generation of today is in a position which enables it to create its own destiny. As to the question of how it can do this while still deriving its inspiration and strength from another culture whose methods and values it has not yet fully assimilated remains the central and baffling question. One fact seems obvious, however: there is no turning away from Europe. This generation's psychological duality, its bilingual, bicultural character are clear manifestations of this fact. It has to judge itself, to choose, and to act in terms of concepts and values rooted not in its own tradition but in a tradition that it has still not fully appropriated.

On the political level, looking reality in the face, one cannot but admit the supremacy of physical force as the final arbiter of political action. But the hope is that one day power in the Arab world will be domesticated and made gentle. What is clear is that we cannot rely on empty forms or accept the consolation of appearances. Whether or not the democratic state is soon established will not settle the fundamental problems nor bring to an end the political challenge facing the younger Arab generation. It is precisely the emotional belief in a final goal which, when reached, will solve everything that numbs the will and renders acceptable what is difficult and confusing in the present.

One often forgets that when hope finally broke forth with the coming of the Arab revolution, it was the here and now which that hope had called the future. But perhaps the strange alchemy in all hope transforms it into something else when it is thwarted. Indeed this is the one pitfall which has caused revolutions to abandon their origins and to end by betraying themselves.

My conviction is that the Arab revolution will not be abandoned or betrayed but that, with the grace of God, it will flower into a new civilization in the Arab world. How can this happen in our time unless the younger Arab generation recognizes its historic task and by a supreme effort of will surpasses itself to create a new destiny in the Middle East?

Islam and Nationalism in Africa

by

William H. Lewis

William H. Lewis is a Research Specialist
and Writer on African Affairs.

Speaking before South Africa's Parliament earlier this year, the Prime Minister of the United Kingdom, Sir Harold Macmillan, indicated that the most striking impression he had formed during his peregrinations through the "Dark Continent" was of the strength of African national consciousness. The Prime Minister pointed out that: "In different places, it may take different forms, but it is happening everywhere. The wind of change is blowing through the continent." Since African national consciousness is a political reality, Sir Harold remonstrated: "Our national policies must take account of it." The Prime Minister went on to conclude: "Of course, you understand this as well as anyone. You are sprung from Europe, the home of nationalism. And here in Africa you have yourselves created a full nation—a new nation. Indeed, in the history of our times yours will be recorded as the first of the African nationalisms."[1]

The winds of change are indeed pouring through the continent, and even the political and racial nationalism of the original white settlers of South Africa now is being overshadowed by the political awakening of Africa's people of color. The Africans' drive for independence, equality and status has been cloaked in many forms—such as messianic movements, tribal revivalism and modern-based nationalist organizations—as well as assumed many modes of expression—including Mau Mau barbarism, passive resistance, boycotts and agitational strife. Whatever the form or the mode of expression, however, the tide of independence is rising, and 1960 has truly become the "year of Africa." Over the course of the next seven months alone, Mali, the Malagasy Republic, the Belgian Congo, Somalia, and

Nigeria are scheduled to gain their independence, bringing to seventeen the number of independent African nations.[2] Even more significantly, perhaps, almost two-thirds of Africa's peoples will have unshackled themselves from the colonial imperium by the declining days of 1960.

Overshadowed in this dramatic welter of political change has been the somewhat less publicized but equally significant spread of Islam through the northern half of tropical Africa. Unlike its nationalist counterpart, however, Islam has deep historical roots in the *Bilād as-Sūdān*. The contact of tropical Africa with Islam was achieved soon after the death of the Prophet Muhammad in 632 A.D. However, this zealously evangelical faith first came to the region in full tide in the eleventh century when Ibn Yasin, a Muslim missionary, established himself as religious proconsul among the southern Berber communities of present-day Mauritania. His followers, known as Almoravids, created a vast empire extending from the Senegal River in the south to Castile in the north. The Almoravids' most important contribution, however, was to anchor Islam in the western Sudanic belt through the conversion of powerful neighboring tribal chieftains. With the subsequent decline of the Almoravids, more powerful Sudanic kingdoms sprang into existence under the Islamic banner. The Mali Empire, which endured from 1050, when its ruling monarch apostasized to Islam, until the fifteenth century, was perhaps the greatest Negro polity to grace the world stage during this period. It was succeeded by another West African kingdom, the Songhai (1468-1591) which provided yet additional impetus to the spread of Islam.[3]

In East Africa, Islamicized tribes have been carrying their religion down the Red Sea coastline and into the Nile Valley since the seventh century. While the Coptic Christian kingdom of Aksum (or Ethiopia) stood as a mountain-locked barrier, the tide of Islam soon swirled past this isolated civilization. In the sixteenth century, a combined Arab-Somali army actually marched almost to the outskirts of Ethiopia's capital only to be defeated and forced back towards the coastal littoral of the Gulf of Aden. Farther to the south, an Arab force established itself at Mombasa in 1696. Subsequently, in 1784, Zanzibar, was conquered and subjugated by the Imam of Muscat and, in 1832, the ruling Imam, Sayyid Sa'id, transferred his capital from the Arabian Peninsula to this gossamer island kingdom. From Zanzibar, Islamic influence penetrated along the coastal reaches of Kenya and Tanganyika, reinforced at the beginning of the twentieth century by the arrival of large numbers of Indian Muslims.

The greatest impetus to Islamic propagation, however, has come from a wholly unanticipated quarter. The European, through the implantation of his political dominion over Africa for more than fifty years, through the seduction of his material culture, the quaint conceits born of his feelings of cultural superiority, the excellence of his bush schools, and by sheer force, has placed in doubt many of the traditional institutions of tribal Africa. He also has created out of whole cloth new cities and towns, mining and industrial complexes, and the sinews of new African classes, elites, and leadership. Concomitantly, Africa has spawned a new breed of man, the disinherited rural proletariat, the town wage earner *cum* political agitator, and the cultural entrepreneur, who serves as a middleman between tribalist and Westerner, interpreting the demands of the modern world to his illiterate brethren. Accompanying the inroads of the West in Africa have been new ideals of progress, unique modes of political expression, shifting loyalties, and value constellations totally divorced from the lore of the past.

Under the European impact, especially in those areas most accessible to Western material influence, the African's traditional religion has often proved of limited value in supplying meaningful solutions for the ubiquitous problems posed by the modern world. While generalization concerning the pantheon of animistic beliefs and rituals which prevailed among Africans at the moment of European interlopement is hazardous, a brief excursus is necessary. As Dr. Trimingham has underlined in his recent West African survey, most Africans have tended to believe that the world about them was created in balance or harmony. Within this universe—which was both harsh and menacing—the role of religion was primarily ritual involving "the action of man to maintain power in equilibrium" and to preserve the "harmony" of the dynamic cosmos.[4] Within this cosmos, the African was "wielded through birth and initiation into a holy community" *in which religion and society were one. Ritual and belief tended to reflect the degree of social integration.*[5] With the widening Western impact, however, traditional religion and African society tended to come unhinged, and the individual African increasingly felt compelled to seek his salvation elsewhere.

In spiritual matters, the African increasingly has turned to Islam, transforming his new religion at the same time that he embraces it into a peculiarly African confession. In areas of more secular urgency, political nationalism, albeit also in transmogrified indigenous raiment, has been eagerly adopted to cover the African's temporal nakedness. When one considers that many Africans are drinking deeply of the wines of Western materialism and nationalism, the limited tapping of the spiritual cask of Christianity seems anomalous, at least upon first glance.

Colonial policy, at least in part, also has played a significant role in the rapid spread of Islam in tropical Africa. In northern Nigeria, for example, the British system of "indirect rule" helped to bolster the flagging fortunes of the Muslim Emirs. By according political preferences to the Fulani rulers of the north, the British reinforced the existing sociopolitical hierarchy, one which was founded on the *jihad* and the holy writ of *Sharī'a* Law. S. F. Nadel has demonstrated that, as a direct result of British colonial support, Islamic law within recent years has gradually been superseding the customary precepts of tribal animism in the Nupe area of Nigeria.[6] At the same time, the ruling Muslim Emirates have tended to take on an "almost fictitious orthodoxy and rigidity in the face of any unwelcome demands or innovations, while the Protecting Power has almost invariably respected this attitude for the willing cooperation" of the Muslim rulers.[7] Thus:

> The policy of indirect rule as interpreted in Nigeria shackled its peoples with the existing ruling class, tied down both Muslims and pagans to the *status quo,* and isolated them from the rest of the world; and although this policy failed since it did not take into account the inevitable encroachments of new forces, it succeeded in so retarding the northern Emirates that they remained stagnant and undeveloped until recent years.[8]

For the bulk of animists, consequently, all hope of salvation before the power of the Emirs has reposed in conversion to Islam. Nadel has shown how in the Nupe tribal community conversion has become almost mandatory due to the application of *Sharīʿa* Law to cases involving customary rights. In addition, apostasy to Islam offers the hope of identification with the Fulani ruling class, with the "social elite, and, by extension, with the power which has become apparent in the Nupe capital" where the bulk of the Fulani overlords reside. In the process, however, Islam has added to the unification of the northern Nigerian conquest-states, "extending the area of a common culture over a population otherwise unified only by political means." Islam, thus, has transformed a binding of peoples together by military coercion in the nineteenth century, into a belonging together—the "conscious belonging together that goes with" a shared religious creed.[9]

Of course, other factors can be adduced for the growing and most singular success of Islam throughout West African regions bordering on Nigeria. This dynamic, extremely plastic religious confession is propagated by Africans among people of color. Thus, it has popular appeal as a fundamentally African religion. In addition, its dogma, while fixed, is nevertheless susceptible to external influences, permitting local beliefs and other accretions to be baptized into the new religion. In its folk manifestations,

Islam does not challenge the underlying beliefs of Africans; rather it frequently reinforces them. Conversion to Islam also is made attractive as a consequence of: (1) the cultural prestige which it brings—as witnessed by opportunity Islam affords for at least a rudimentary education in remote rural areas; (2) the social integration it offers—in a world increasingly fragmented by the Western impact Islam extends the individual African an opportunity to anchor himself to new corporate institutions; and (3) the comforting religious values it embraces—in that Islam purports to provide assured solutions to the problems both of this world and the next. Apropos this question, Christian evangelism probably has contributed as much impetus to the processes of Islamization through its rigidity, internal contradictions, and perpetuation of inferiority-superiority complexes, as it has provided illumination of the Christian way.

While no accurate data are available relating to the number and rate of conversions in Africa south of the Sahara, some consensus obtains among qualified observers that Islam has burst out of the Sahara hinterland and the savannah regions of West Africa and is now making rapid inroads in the central and coastal rain-forest belt. In the Belgian Congo, for example, the number of Muslims has ballooned to more than 100,000.[10] In former French West Africa, over eight million Muslims have been counted, while in excess of twelve million populate both northern and southern Nigeria. To the East, over six million Muslims inhabit what is commonly accepted as the Horn area, and more than three million are presently residing in Kenya, Uganda, Tanganyika and Mozambique. In more meaningful terms, perhaps, it might be noted that, by the declining days of 1960, the affairs of at least ten of Africa's seventeen independent nations will be presided over by Muslim statesmen.

The political ramifications of Islam's spread have been viewed by some Western "Africanists" over the past several years with grave concern. Many profess to see serious international power problems in the possible emergence of a Muslim

African "bloc" which would enhance Afro-Asian neutralist voting strength before the United Nations, as well as at general international conferences. Some observers also express considerable perturbation over the possibility of an extension of disproportionate UAR throughout the African continent. Others simply experience and manifest varying degrees of traumatic shock at the prospect of growing Muslim power in world councils at the seeming expense of the once much-heralded Western monopoly of power.

Such an approach subsumes a degree of political, social and cultural unity among African Muslims which is more apparent than real. Numerous deep-seated cleavages exist within the Islamic community which, *inter alia*, are predicated upon: 1) traditional tribal and ethnic rivalries; 2) diverse racial backgrounds; 3) differences in degree of religiosity, as well as in ritual practices; 4) clashing class and special economic interests—as between Syrian-Lebanese traders and local African merchants; 5) membership in competing religious confraternities (*turuq*); and 6) marked variations in degree of Westernization. In addition, European colonial regimes have erected trans-territorial barriers of their own which deeply impede efforts to create broad political groupings. One might mention at this juncture some of the more obvious impedimenta: 1) differing official languages and administrative operational procedures; 2) fundamental dichotomies in outlook with regard to the responsibilities and needs of government; and 3) different currencies, marketing systems, and patterns of trade and commerce. These barriers are not easily overcome by the unifying influences which may exist in African Islam.

Nor, for that matter, is Islam so firmly entrenched in most territories that it has become the "national religion" of emergent states. The complex situation obtaining in West Africa probably best illustrates this point. In the Western region, European empire-builders erected states in the nineteenth and early twentieth centuries at right angles to major African culture zones.

The culture zones extend horizontally on an east-west axis, while the European colonial powers tended to create new national entities on a north-south orbit. As a result, each emergent West African state today contains a "cross-section of very different cultural patterns, ranging from the predominantly Negroid groups in the tropical forest on the coast to the predominantly Sudanic groups in the open savannah in the north."[11] Only in Mauritania, and possibly Niger—among the territories of the former French West African Federation—has Islam become sufficiently entrenched to be accepted as the "national religion." Even in Mauritania, profound ethnic and cultural cleavages between the Arabic-speaking northern Moors and the riverain Negro Toucouleurs (*Takrur*) in the south have not been completely submerged by the Islamic veil which curtains the entire Mauritanian population. (Apropos this point, it is interesting to note that the Toucouleurs themselves have a low regard for their Negro Wolof co-religionists inhabiting the region across the Senegal River because of the laxity of the latter's religious practices and beliefs.)

In Mali (Soudan and Senegal), as well as Guinea, Islam has become the predominant faith of numerous Africans. However, it is not a universally accepted faith. Consequently, heavy reliance upon Islam, "in party ideologies or propaganda, as a basis for political solidarity, could have the effect of dividing people more than it united them."[12] Probably nowhere in Africa is this fact more clearly portrayed than in the Chad, where ethno-religious cleavages between the Muslim communities of the north and the Christian-animist-Bantu south pose serious problems for national unity and political stability.

The north is relatively more backward and given to the perpetuation of tribal traditionalism, as well as religious conservatism. In the past, its leadership has been relatively weak and divided by personality clashes which impeded sustained, united action. However, on February 1, 1960, the north's five heterogeneous political formations amalgamated into the *Parti National Africain* (PNA) under the leadership of Ahmad Koulamallah.

Its essential goals are the maintenance of "Muslim tradition" in educational and social matters and the loosening of political ties with France concomitant with the strengthening of relations with adjacent Muslim territories. The relatively advanced and politically sophisticated south, however, is more inclined to challenge tribal conservatism and to adopt programs favoring secularization of education and social advance. The present government is controlled by the *Parti Progressiste Tchadien* (PPT-RDA) which represents the interests of the more progressive south, a region unalterably opposed to national unification with neighboring Muslim states. As issues such as these become joined in the very near future, considerable political effervescence and disabling intercommunal strife can be anticipated to the likely detriment of the Chad's national stability.

On the other hand, the situation in the Cameroun Republic, a former French trust territory which acquired its independence on January 1, 1960, is somewhat anomalous. Here, the seeming political homogeneity of the Islamic northern region, the moderate outlook of its Muslim leadership, and the profound cleavages and incompatibilities of the more advanced Christian-animist southern coastal communities, have produced a remarkable situation in which the nation's most conservative elements are primarily responsible for the preservation of the Republic's unity and stability. At the time of independence, the Cameroun's Prime Minister, Ahmadu Ahidjo, inherited a litany of serious difficulties highlighted by widespread civil strife inspired by the outlawed *Union des Populations Camerounaise* (UPC), as well as economic and social unrest among the Bamileke tribesmen of the southwest, and spasmodic feuding among local politicians in Douala and Yaounde. In the intervening period, Prime Minister Ahidjo has been able to maintain a delicate balance between his Muslim supporters in the north—who account for one-third of the total population—and the relatively more advanced coastal communities. A Fulani by birth, Ahidjo was educated in Yaounde and entered political life by joining a southern party which numbered among its leaders many of the nation's Catholic intellectuals. In 1958, however, Ahidjo formed his own party, *l'Union Camerounaise* (UC), an organization having basic roots in the north but which is making strenuous efforts to extend its influence into the coastal regions.

At present, the Prime Minister of the Cameroun Republic is serving as a political hyphen between Muslim north and Christian-animist south. With patience and considerable forebearance, he is attempting to establish a meaningful universe of discourse in a deeply divided West African land, one in which disagreements will be acted out and resolved in legislative assemblies rather than in the accidental, bloody encounters of army patrols and terrorist bands. In the process, Ahmadu Ahidjo is seeking to demonstrate that the conservative Muslim north can serve as a leavening political influence as the Republic searches for the correct path to an awakening "national consciousness" and eventual unity of effort.[13]

It is not entirely inconceivable that a comparable situation might arise in Nigeria, where major political dichotomies in the more advanced Yoruba and Ibo south (between the N.C.N.C. and the Action Group) could afford the Muslim north an opportunity to assume a similar lodestar role. Thus, here too, positions would be reversed and conservative Islamic groups—willing to make some concessions to modernism—may ultimately be compelled to moderate differences between the followers of Azikwe and Awolowo and, at the same time, seek to consolidate the bonds of an embryonic Nigerian national federation.

For much of Africa, however, the representatives of conservative Islamic groups are unlikely to encounter numerous opportunities for the assumption of such profitable, reassuring roles. Under the Western colonial impact, a new political geography has been imposed, the sacredness of old tribal cultures has been partially despoiled, and new African political elites have emerged in the crucible of colonial dominion. These new elites do not depend upon genealogical ties for ascriptive status, but emphasize instead achievements engendered by education, as well as inborn organizational ability. They seek to channel political activity outside the rules and procedures instituted by traditional society over the centuries to guide and to limit political action. Thus, in essence, the newly emergent political elites are changing the rules of the game—at least as it has been played in the past. Their goal is to mobilize African society behind efforts to fashion new institutions—as well as to disentangle the old—to formulate a more meaningful ideology with which to meet the problems of the twentieth century, and to marshal national resources, both physical and human, for a frontal assault upon the existing barriers to modernism.

The new religion of these elites is African nationalism, the appeal of which rests upon common experience with Western value systems, however variant. The strength, character, and appeal of this new secular religion often rest upon the charismatic qualities of leaders such as Kwame Nkrumah, Felix Houphouet-Boigny, Sekou Touré, Julius Nyere, and Mamadou Dia. If there is a messianic quality in the appeal of these Africans, it is in their ability to inculcate overwhelming numbers of their fellow Africans and to secure mass support for essentially temporal goals. As one recent observer has noted: "The situation has been right for the emergence of such charismatic leaders; the assertion of African aspirations has required symbols which these men and their movements have provided."[14]

Mass movements, a new phenomenon in Africa, are of particular significance for the evolution of nationalism in the continent since they have developed into the handmaidens of the emerging political elite. It is through these movements that policy decisions ultimately affecting the orientation of national governments are struck, territorial support elicited, and that the largest number of Africans gain experience in the building of a sense of "membership in an African state." The aim of these nationalist movements is to cut across diverse loyalties whether they are tribal, racial or religious. In the case of Islam, they seek to reduce its far-reaching influence upon political loyalties to as negligible a level as possible. Recently in Ghana, for example, the formation and perpetuation of a Muslim Association Party provoked strong hostility from Prime Minister Nkrumah and his Convention People's Party. The CPP has vigorously sought to sublimate religious differences for the sake of political unity. As a result, the Muslim Association Party is a moribund organization today.

Thus, nationalism in contemporary tropical Africa confronts Islam with a challenge which is almost as old as the history of religion. As invoked by modern secularists, nationalism is anathema to orthodox Muslim theology since it questions what is at the very core of Islam. For example, African nationalism raises the fundamental issue of Islam's role as a political as well as a religious formative influence and questions whether or not it is capable of rapid adjustment to the dictates and exigencies of the "modern world." Indeed, can religious authoritarianism be subordinated to the authoritarianism of temporal nationalism? Is Islam capable of accepting an almost Augustinian opposition of the heavenly and the earthly? Can nationalist absolutism, with its principle of mass inclusion and its preferred role as custodian of the past and master of Africa's destiny, compromise with Muslim reformists? More crucially, perhaps, can Islam's reformers compromise with leaders who are more concerned with the meeting of today's material needs than with the geography of human souls on the morrow?

Guinea serves as an excellent illustration of the relationship of the points at issue. Nationalism as an expression of the African's search for identity, new status, and dignity is in full flood in contemporary Guinea. Under the leadership of Sekou Touré, himself a Muslim, Guinea opted for independence during the September, 1958, referendum held throughout French Africa on President Charles de Gaulle's Constitution of the Fifth Republic. In essence, Guinea voted against membership in the rapidly evolving French Community. Having severed its former colonial umbilical cord, the leaders of this small African state have sought to establish new roots for themselves in the international community. Dilatoriness and hesitation on the part of the Western world in affording Guinea diplomatic recognition permitted the Soviet bloc to hasten to fill a dreaded vacuum—that of isolation and lack of international status. In need of recognition, technical aid, and large-scale assistance in creating necessary administrative services, Guinea accepted Soviet blandishments with alacrity. However, to counter the impact of this action upon the West, as well as to underscore Guinea's neutralist foreign policy, loose ties were established with Ghana in a vaguely defined, embryonic political "union." Despite the overwhelmingly Islamic confession of its indigenous population, the Guinea Government also has hastened to establish diplomatic and other ties with Israel from which it is hoped that some inspiration for the economic advance of an undeveloped society will be gleaned.

The basic fact of life for the existing Guinean leadership is the impoverishment of the bulk of the country's more than two million people. As Sekou Touré has underscored, there is no Western nation which has found itself in recent years in the same human condition as is encountered in most African states.

> Populations which include more than 80 per cent . . . illiterate peasants, with an annual individual income of less than $100, and, therefore, with the most precarious conditions of life—these are the harsh realities of Africa, when it is no longer masked behind the ridiculous veil of exoticism which hides from unaware eyes the colossal misery of our vast underdeveloped countries at present sparsely populated because of centuries of slavery.

Within this harsh environment, the Guinean leader is not without hope:

> And yet in this poverty, of which humanity should be ashamed, there is man with his invincible faith in the destiny of humanity; there is his hope, his determination to win and to grow; his immense thirst for brotherhood and har-

mony, his kindness still in its purest form; and, at the same
time, his extraordinary energy and sharp sense of responsibility. . . .[15]

In an apparent effort to harness the drives and ambitions of
Guineans, political life has been focused upon the country's primary nationalist organization, the *Parti Democratique de Guinée*
(PDG), whose *leitmotiv* is complete independence combined
with popular action. As the so-called brain of the state, the PDG
serves as the medium through which the "general will" of
Guineans is to seek expression. Indeed, no important governmental decision may be taken without the prior approval of the
PDG, or more properly, its National Political Bureau. Once consensus is attained, however, all sectors of the national population are expected to cooperate in the implementation of PDG
policy decisions.

The present-day action goals of the PDG are essentially revolutionary. The Party clearly seeks an early termination of all
former colonial connections, profound social and economic reforms directed from the center, the transformation of tribal
communities into modern political societies as quickly as possible, and the creation of a strong, socialist-oriented central
government. The existing leadership, as exemplified by President
Touré himself, accepts Marxist ideology only in so far as it
"applies to present conditions in Africa"—i.e., to the struggle
against colonialism and the processes of decolonization.[16] Illustra-
tive of the PDG's distinctively African approach to Marxist
doctrine is its tendency to reject the concept of class warfare.
While recognizing that some marked differences obtain between
social classes, these differences are held to be insignificant when
compared with those prevailing between colonized peoples and
the colonizers. The PDG's main concern is the mobilization of
all classes in the struggle against colonialism and poverty.

While the PDG tends to respect divergent social, cultural and
religious customs—and it should be remembered that over twenty
tribal languages are spoken in Guinea today—it seeks, at the

same time, to level all existing barriers to modernization. Thus, while it may organize festivities on the occasion of a Muslim holiday, the PDG concomitantly will seek to eliminate those tribal and religious obstacles which impede the advancement of Muslim women. For example, within recent months it has been pursuing an active campaign against polygamy, marriages before religious clerics, and divorce without satisfactory manifest cause. To those preservers of custom and religious guardians of Muslim tradition in the Futa Jalon region who vibrantly oppose the toppling of the lore of the past, the PDG offers only ultimate capitulation or banishment. Where orthodox and folk Islam interpose spiritual reservations to the secular road selected for material progress, they are likely to be received as the obscurantist remnants of a decadent civilization. On the other hand, where African Islam proves malleable and plastic, no longer anxious simply to underpin regional ethnocentricities, it may well serve as a leavening influence and force making for unity of action.

Elsewhere in Africa the struggle against Islamic obscurantism is not yet entirely joined. However, the issues are becoming increasingly, almost painfully, evident. They are most apparent, perhaps, in Senegal where the present debate between African nationalism and traditional Islam is most intense. Led by religious holy men (*marabouts*) *cum* politicians, traditional Islam has found its strongest expression under the inspiration of the *Parti de la Solidarité Senegalaise* (PSS). In a state where tribal chieftains have wielded little power, the influence of the *marabouts* upon the political affairs of local communities has been extensive—occasionally, all-pervasive. Under the leadership of the Grand Marabout of Kaolack, El Hadj Ibrahim Niasse, Senegal's religious elite has jealously sought to safeguard its political privileges and spiritual prerogatives. In particular, it has cast a baneful eye upon the territory's leading nationalist organization, the *Union Progressiste Senegalaise* (UPS), which has espoused a program of extensive social and economic reforms. In the past, the UPS has been publicly branded as an enemy of

Islam and, as recently as June, 1959, the *maraboutical* elite under Cheikh Tidjani Sy provoked grave demonstrations in the region of Tivaouane against the government headed by the UPS nationalists.

For Senegal's Prime Minister, Mamadou Dia, himself a Muslim who has recently returned from a pilgrimage to Mecca, the opposition of the conservative *marabouts* has been a cause for some substantial perturbation. He remains convinced, however, that his belief in secular progress for the "masses" is the only means of raising Senegal to higher status in the community of nations. The tenacity with which Mamadou Dia and his colleagues cling to their programs of action appears, finally, to be producing some success. On January 13, 1960, the PSS extended the olive branch of reconciliation, thus terminating for the present a major skirmish between the defenders of conservative Islam and the proponents of modern nationalism. Despite this detente, however, the fundamental issue involving the proper role to be assigned Islam in the modern nation remains to be more fully debated and resolved.

Until the confrontation between Islam and nationalism is finally acted out, it would appear that religion in Africa south of the Sahara may prove as much a divisive factor as a unifying influence. If Islam is to serve as a positive force for greater African unity, at least in the near future, its greatest appeal is likely to be predicated upon the emotional appeal it conjures up from the history of the great Islamic empires and states which abided in Africa in centuries past. Part of this memory is reflected in the creation of the modern Federation of Mali, which takes its name from the fourteenth-century West African kingdom. As Thomas Hodgkin has so ably pointed out, a number of political leaders in this region contend today that "if African governments have constructed large, and relatively durable, political systems in the past, they can do so again, under the changed conditions of the present".[17] The PDG, for example, is inspired—in part at least—by nineteenth-century empire-building movements which were "Muslim in inspiration and outlook." Mass organizations, Guinea's PDG see themselves as the successor of "these system-building, anticolonial, reforming movements" of the nineteenth century. However, one fundamental difference exists. Contemporary African nationalist movements frequently are secularist, modernist, and Marxian in approach. Thus, even here the main strands of African history have been caught up in the profound social, economic and political changes which are sweeping through the continent today. These changes can offer little solace or comfort to the defenders of conservative Islam in Africa south of the Sahara.

Conclusion

Prediction is always a hazardous undertaking. In Africa, where the pace of change has been constantly accelerating, this observation is doubly valid. Indeed, it is not without reason that the continent is crudely shaped along the lines of a gigantic question-mark.

Moreover, we are observing Africa at a moment when its indigenous peoples are becoming increasingly able to shape their own destinies. As C. Wright Mills recently has pointed out, while all men are free to make history, some men are manifestly freer than others. At present, the bulk of African leaders wish to avoid becoming "the utensils of history." As a result, human behavior in this part of the world is not likely always to conform to previous patterns.

Nevertheless, with some considerable trepidation, I would offer the following predictions:

1. Islam will continue to register growing success in its evangelistic efforts throughout many regions of tropical Africa. The areas of greatest penetration during the coming decade will probably embrace Upper Volta, the Ivory Coast, Sierra Leone, and portions of the Belgian Congo, former French Equatorial Africa, Tanganyika, and Mozambique.

2. Despite these successes, tribalism and nationalism are likely to prove more potent forces in Africa than religion. Thus, while Islam will continue to proceed from victory to victory on the spiritual plane, its effectiveness as a political force probably will go into eclipse.

3. In an effort to reinforce and reinvigorate itself, African Islam is likely to establish broader ties with the Arab world. Indeed, the process of religious adaptation and reinterpretation which has been in full flow in the Near East may well prove instructive to the guardians of the Islamic tradition south of the Sahara.

4. On the political level, the vertical relationships erected during the colonial period in Africa will be supplanted by constantly changing horizontal relationships. By this I mean to imply that African nationalism will be transformed into a type of "quasi-nationalism" as new combinations of states evolve, dissolve and reform.

Thus, we shall witness efforts at federation or other forms of union in (a) the Horn area (b) Senegambia (c) Mali and neighbors (d) the *Entente* (Niger, Dahomey, Upper Volta, Ivory Coast), Equatorial Africa (Gabon, Cameroun, Chad, Central African Republic), and elsewhere.

5. Finally, the Negro-Arab myth will be exploded as newly independent North African and tropical African states develop communities of economic interest and areas of political discourse. Color and the Sahara will prove illusory barriers as Africans find their continent shrinking under the stimulus of common needs, wants and expectations.

---

1. Cited in *West Africa*, February 6, 1960, p. 144.
2. Already independent are Liberia, Ghana, Guinea, Togo, Cameroun, Morocco, Tunisia, Libya, the United Arab Republic, the Sudan, the Ethiopian Empire and the Union of South Africa.
3. For an excellent review of this period, see J. S. Trimingham, *Islam in West Africa* (London: Oxford University Press, 1959); S. F. Nadel, *A Black Byzantium* (London: Oxford University Press, 1942); Arthur Pellegrim, *L'Islam dans le Monde* (Paris: Payot, 1955); G. Parrinder,

Religion in an African City (London: Oxford University Press, 1953) and M. Cardaire, "L'Islam et la cellule sociale Africaine" in *L'Afrique et l'Asie,* No. 29 (First Quarter, 1955).

4. Trimingham, *op. cit.,* p. 6.
5. In traditional societies, Daryll Forde has pointed out in *African Worlds,* (London: International African Institute, 1954) that, the greater the economic self-sufficiency and the political freedom of action of localized groups, the greater was the "segmentation of ritual activity and the particularism of the objects of worship." On the other hand, the closer the integration of economic activity and of social control among African groups, the more tightly integrated were basic social concepts and ritual forms.
6. S. F. Nadel, *op. cit.,* pp. 755-774.
7. J. N. D. Anderson, *Islamic Law in Africa* (London: H.M. Stationary Office, 1954), p. 219.
8. Trimingham, *op. cit.,* p. 205.
9. S. F. Nadel, *Nupe Religion* (London: Routledge, 1954). An excellent treatise which comes directly to grips with Muslim influence in one West African Area.
10. *Le Courrier d'Afrique* (Leopoldville), July 28, 1955.
11. See James Coleman, *Togoland* (International Conciliation, September, 1956).
12. These points are clearly defined by the eminent African specialist, Thomas Hodgkin, in his address, "Political Forces in French West Africa," delivered at Berkeley, California, March 29, 1960.
13. The Ahidjo Government has registered some notable gains in recent months as was made evident during the April, 1960, elections for Cameroun's first post-independence National Assembly. The Premier and his supporters won sixty of 100 seats while the largest single opposition group, the UPC, acquired only twenty-two. However, a government majority is almost assured as a result of the absence of any contest for the forty-four seats reserved in the Muslim north which went to the UC.
14. Dr. F. X. Sutton in a paper submitted before the Social Science Research Council, Gould House, June 8-12, 1959, has covered this point in depth.
15. President Toure in an address before the United Nations on November 5, 1959.
16. See George Fischer, "Quelques aspects de la doctrine politique guineene," *Civilisations,* IX (1959), 457-478.
17. Hodgkin, *Ibid.*

Prospects
for a
United Maghrib

by

William Sands

William Sands is Director of Publications of
the Middle East Institute and Editor of the
Middle East Journal.

What is the *Maghrib?* The Arabic word itself, by origin or by extension, can mean a number of things, but, generally speaking, it means the western land—of the Arabs, that is, and therefore the extreme northwest of the African continent. In a general way the term Maghrib has been applied to all of North Africa west of Egypt, that is, Libya, Tunisia, Algeria and Morocco. The King of Morocco has on a number of occasions specifically included the Spanish Sahara and the new "Islamic Republic of Mauretania" of the French Community in a *"Maghrib Irredenta,"* extending as far south, indeed, as St. Louis de Sénégal. The President of Tunisia has said that "we shall again be one country from Sallum to Casablanca," that is, from Cyrenaica in Libya to the Atlantic.

I shall exclude both Libya and the territories to the south of the present borders of Morocco, for the purposes of the "model," as the economists say. In so doing, I exclude as well any extensive personal experience in what I have to say, for my only time in residence in North Africa was in Tripolitania. I am aware as well that joint communiqués following King Muhammad V's recent visits to Eastern Arab states included a reference to Mauretania as being in the same status of Arab territory unjustly held as that of Palestine and Algeria.

Then, before we proceed to the discussion of the unity of the Maghrib as such, we ought to examine the degree to which the people of the area respond to another and ecumenical idea. This is the "Arab nation," the concept of one people and one country which stretches from the Atlantic Ocean to the Persian Gulf. On this matter we have one clear official statement. The Tunisian

Constitution of June 1, 1959, refers to "Tunisian membership in the Arab community." The language, it seems to me, makes the point clear, especially when it is considered in conjunction with wording in the same section on the unity of the Maghrib, to be discussed below. The plurality of the Arab world, as "members," is what is stressed, not the idea of a unit.

Of the three Arab "members" we are considering here, the Algerians represented by the National Liberation Front (FLN) have had perhaps the closest ties with the Eastern Arabs. The support which the FLN has received from the United Arab Republic (UAR) and Iraq, to name only two, may have done something to predispose its leaders to close ties with these Eastern Arabs after an independence they hope to gain. But there is little doubt that, as of now, FLN goals, insofar as they are other than purely Algerian in character, are principally North African. There have, furthermore, been numerous recent reports of a cooling in relations between FLN leaders and the UAR, but these are not confirmable so far as I am concerned. The principal point remains the North African character to the movement.

As for Morocco and total Arab unity, the recent visit of King Muhammad V to the eastern Arab states was a gesture of friendship—it has little to do with unity. Indeed, the phrase in the Moroccan-Iraqi joint communiqué issued in Baghdad on February 3, 1960, concerning "strengthening the Arab League and seeking to amend its charter on the basis of respect for every member state . . ." would seem to indicate little enthusiasm on the part of Moroccan rulers for any Casablanca-to-Basrah Arab unity in the near future.

Given these attitudes toward unity of all the Arabs, what are the positions of the two governments and of the Algerian people toward the narrower union of the Maghrib as we have defined it? I may say here, parenthetically, that on the basis of all the evidence I have seen, I accept the position of the National Liberation Front as representing that of the great majority of the Algerian people. The response is practically unanimous. I do not know of a single national leader in any of the three countries who has not enthusiastically endorsed the idea that the Maghrib should again be one. Of the three countries, the position of Tunisia has been the most formalized. Adherence to "the unity of the Greater Maghrib" is part of the preamble of the 1959 constitution referred to above, as a solemn resolution of the Tunisian people. Article 2 of the General Provisions of the constitution declares the Tunisian republic to be an "integral part" of the greater Maghrib, and asserts that it is the duty of the state to strive for the achievement of the unity of the Maghrib. The original wording of Article 2 specifically posited that Tunisia might forego some part of its sovereignty in order to enter into such a union. This wording was not specifically retained, but there is little doubt that Tunisians might be so willing. President Habib Bourguiba (Buraqibah) has long been known as one of the most ardent spokesmen for the proposition and is frequently mentioned as a possible head of a federal government.

Insofar as the Algerians are concerned, the proceedings of the Tangier Convention of April 27-30, 1958, in which representatives of the FLN took part with Tunisians and Moroccans, offer the clearest statement of their attitude toward unity. The convention resolved:

1. That achievement of Maghrib unity was the goal of all of them.

2. That federation was the best means of achieving it.

3. That a consultative assembly made up of the three national assemblies should be convoked to consider matters of federal and common interest during a transitional period.

4. That the three governments should refrain from making any basic international agreements on matters of foreign policy or defense until the federal institutions envisaged above could be put into effect. It is well known, of course, that the provisional Algerian government of Farhat 'Abbas operates from Tunisian

soil and that a great part of its support comes from Tunisia and Morocco. So much so, that this past April we saw the renewal of incidents between France and Tunisia with the French seeming once again to claim the right of "hot pursuit" against Algerian rebel forces operating from Tunisian soil.

The attitude of the Moroccan government is equally clear. Although the *Istiqlal* party which represented Morocco at the 1958 Tangier Convention is now split in two, both the right wing out of power and the left wing in power remain dedicated to the proposition of a united Maghrib. Since Morocco is still, in theory—and to a great extent, in fact—an absolute monarchy, the position of King Muhammad V toward the concept becomes of major importance. On August 20, 1958, in a speech commemorating the fifth anniversary of his exile to Madagascar by the French, the King listed what he considered to be the prime national objectives of Morocco. Among these was a Maghribi union in which he specifically included Algeria.

It is not astonishing that there should be this unanimity. These three peoples have shared unity in history still meaningful to all of them. Two great empires, led by indigenous Berber dynasties, ruled over most of North Africa and part of Spain for more than two hundred years, and their names are still famous. The Almoravids (*al-Murabti*), with their origin in the territories around the Niger that are now considered "Morocco Irredenta," founded the city of Marrakesh in the eleventh century and ruled brilliantly, as far as Algiers to the east, and even for a while in Tunis. They were followed in the twelfth century by the dynasty, also Moroccan, of the Almohades (*al-Muwahhidun,* or "Unitarians"), whose capital was the magnificent Seville and who ruled as far east as the borders of Egypt, until the thirteenth century.

Of what order of magnitude in comparison with other nations would a modern version of the Maghrib be? In sheer area, major. The number of square miles of territory would be something like 1.8 million (it is not possible to be precise, since Morocco's boundaries are not defined). This is more than half the size of the continental United States and as large, approximately, as Argentina. It should be pointed out, however, that about two-thirds of the area is composed of the Southern Territories of Algeria, almost totally desertic in character. The population of such a Maghrib would be in the neighborhood of 23 or 24 million, according to recent estimates, of which that of Algeria and Morocco would be roughly equal and that of Tunisia somewhat more than a third of each. On the African continent the Maghrib would be second in numbers only to Nigeria—about to become independent—and almost exactly the same as Egypt, not including Asian Syria as part of the United Arab Republic.

And what are the present prospects that this kind of Maghrib will come to be? It seems to me that there are two major problems; let us consider them in the order in which they must be solved, if a union is to take place.

The obvious one is the status of Algeria. The central position, the great bulk of the territory and somewhat less than half the prospective population are there. Since November 1, 1954, the National Liberation Front has carried on continuous warfare for an independent Algeria and, until recently, successive French governments have continued to insist that the territory is an integral part of France and cannot be considered *disponible*. They have adduced the presence of some one million Europeans in Algeria as a major reason for not "abandoning" the territory to the nine million indigenous Muslim Algerians. The Algerian response as expressed by the FLN is simpler: Algeria is not France; it has its own existence which must be given expression in the form of an independent state. My own opinion, again, is that by all the logic of modern history, there is no doubt that some ninety per cent of the Algerians are not Frenchmen; that they have a perfect right to express that fact in independence, that independence is what they want, and that Algeria does not become part of France by *fiat*.

If any one man holds the key to the solution of the problem,

it is President de Gaulle. Brought into power by a near-rebellion
of the army and settlers in Algeria just two years ago, last winter
he became ruler of France by decree, after another abortive
attempt of Europeans in Algeria to force their own will upon
the *Métropole*. General de Gaulle has never associated himself
with the position that there existed no difference between Algeria
and Metropolitan France, but, until last fall, he had presented
no solution of his own. What he has proposed is "self-determination" for Algeria, *after* the complete victory of French arms.
De Gaulle has posed three possible results of an inquiry on
Algerian wishes:

1. Complete integration into France.
2. Complete independence.
3. An association—federal or otherwise—with France, which
would involve some degree of local autonomy.

The General is on record as believing that the first is not practical, that the second would be disastrous and that only the third
offers real hope for settlement. But on another occasion he is
reported to have stated that what he wishes is "the most French
solution" of the crisis, a Delphic kind of pronouncement which
the Europeans of Algeria would almost certainly take to mean
integration. On his New York visit (April 25, 1960) he referred
to the war in Algeria as sad and useless; at San Francisco two
days later he said that the time had passed when one people
could impose its will upon another. What is not clear is whether
he considers Algerians to be "another people," or an amalgam
to which it is difficult to apply the principle.

There is no sign that either party will give up its major
tenet; the Algerians, that they will negotiate only on the manner
in which self-determination is to be implemented and the French,
that there be a final military decision. The latter have recently
stepped up their campaign against the FLN forces, but the prospect of complete victory does not seem nearer, particularly when
the rebel forces are able to operate from the safe haven of
Tunisian and Moroccan territory.

This we know; the rest is speculation. I can only repeat my own conviction that the Algerians will eventually be independent and that, when they are, they will seek closer union with their fellow North Africans. This is, by far, the first and greatest "if."

The second conjecture is—what kind of a union for the Maghrib once united? This latter may seem unimportant now, but if past histories of attempts to federate are any guide, one problem stands out, to my mind, above all. That is the question of a monarchical *versus* a republican form of government. One might say that, for the kind of first steps proposed by the Tangier Conference mentioned above, the problem does not arise. And it is true that there exist federations of sorts that include republics and monarchies. Two come to mind: the British Commonwealth and the United Arab States, but neither of them, I think, corresponds to the degree of unity North Africans are seriously considering for themselves.

Muhammad V of Morocco has been the symbol of liberation for—insofar as it is possible to judge—the great majority of Moroccans. Traditionally, he combines—and certain recent warrants for arrest for *lèse majesté* show that the theory is not dead—both a religious and a secular position that could hardly be subordinated to any other head of a Maghrib federation. He has stated repeatedly that he wishes to guide his people into representative forms of government, but it is clear that the eventual aim is constitutional monarchy.

President Habib Bourguiba, of Tunisia, is the other best-known of North African leaders. During the brief period that Tunisia was still a monarchy after independence, he did not bother to conceal his contempt of the Husayn dynasty and his preference for republican institutions. This preference is now an integral part of the constitution: "We . . . proclaim that the republican order of government is the best guarantee of human rights and the establishment of equality . . . and of promoting the means of public welfare. . . ." Although Bourguiba leads the unit of the prospective federation smallest in size and population, he would be, without doubt, a powerful influence on such a grouping if it came into being within the span of his active years.

The background of the leaders of the FLN is equally republican in character, influenced as they are, practically all of them, by their French education and background. One hears nothing of a revival of the *mystique* of the famed 'Abd al-Qadir, Prince of Algiers at the time of the French conquest, though his descendants in Damascus and France are numerous.

All this is not to say that compromise is not possible. Muhammad V, in his projects for forthcoming popular participation in Moroccan governmental processes, speaks of this development as "republican" in nature. (The word in Arabic for the idea he has in mind is *jamhuri,* which can mean "republican," but there is little doubt that what he means by this word is "popular.") Tunisians and Algerians might accept a chief of state who had a royal designation. This problem will be theirs to work out when the basic one is resolved. The underlying fact, as I see it, is that some sort of union of the Maghrib is one of the probabilities of our political generation.

Patterns of Recent Economic Development in the Arab States

by

Albert J. Meyer

Albert J. Meyer is Associate Director of the
Center for Middle Eastern Studies at Harvard
University.

There is now sufficient evidence to permit a series of defensible generalizations on the patterns of economic development under way in the Arab East. These data emerge from studies by governments, private agencies and collections by the United Nations. Most require discounting in varying degree. Yet even after adjustment there is widespread agreement on the following trends:

First, the extremely rapid growth, in national income terms, which has punctuated the decade and a half since 1945, seems continuing in many countries. Iraq, until recently, and Kuwait, Syria and Lebanon are still adding to net per capita incomes at more than 3 per cent yearly. The astronomical increases made by oil-producing states after 1950 have shrunk. Bad weather recently has cost Syria and Lebanon dearly. But nevertheless, national incomes in these countries are continuing to rise, after adjustment for population increase and inflation, at a vigorous rate.

Jordan and Egypt show much more modest successes—1 per cent or less net per year by most calculations. Overpopulated, resource poor, with tremendous historical obstacles to overcome, these nations cannot hope to equal the rates of growth of their better endowed neighbors to the north and east. Saudi Arabia, for better or worse, remains outside these generalizations. There, we know the oil revenues and a bit about the non-oil sectors of the economy. But until somebody decides whether the peninsula's population is two million or ten million, division of these numbers into annual oil earnings remains an aimless task—even for economists.

Libya and Algeria, moreover, seem on the threshold of tremendous spurts in national income. Export of a million barrels of oil per day from each country three years hence could mean $300 million each in annual income. This would be $300 per capita in Libya and $30 per capita in Algeria per year. Incomes in each country are estimated at about $100 per capita today, so chances for growth are great. A part of the forthcoming oil-induced prosperity will doubtless also cross frontiers into Tunisia and Morocco—through labor force migration and government earnings from pipeline transit fees.

Next, the growth described above remains lumpy, in terms of the living standard of the mass of people. The more sophisticated countries in the Levant, Lebanon and Syria, have seen rising incomes generally. So has Kuwait, which has launched an incredibly effective attack on mass poverty and ignorance. Yet most Iraqis have only begun recently to feel (albeit a small part of) the elation besetting national income statisticians in the country for a decade. Relatively few Saudis have as yet benefited substantially from oil earnings in the kingdom. Jordan and Egypt hover around a per capita income of just over $100 yearly, and overpopulation still makes most citizens count their improvements in spiritual and emotional terms rather than physical.

Third, evidence of the past fifteen years suggests tremendous improvement in the capacities of decision-makers—public and private—to make intelligent investment decisions and to operate enterprises once they are established. Lebanon and Syria have seen considerable factory growth since World War II. Iraq has performed the sizable feat of taming the Tigris and Euphrates rivers and thus paved the way for collateral growth throughout its economy. Contracting has approached a high level of skill throughout the Northern Arab countries. Egypt has run the Suez Canal in a manner to confound the post-1956 Cassandras and now seems intent on a vigorous program of industrial development. Libya is striking hard bargains (typified by time limits on exploration agreements) with oil companies and also seems inclined toward future tax-royalty expenditures which will profit from experience of the Eastern Arabs. There even seem to be stirrings of domestic entrepreneurship around the oil camps in Arabia, and efforts are under way to rationalize the public finance of the kingdom.

Next, oil remains the greatest catalytic agent in area-wide economic growth. The $1.25 billion now being paid yearly by oil companies to eastern Arab producing states continues to have incalculable effect in these countries and residual effect elsewhere. Libya and Algeria each seem destined for at least $300 million annually within the next five years if production forecasts prove true. These revenues make possible rapid installation of social overhead facilities and aid creation of an investment climate for private funds. That climate, while improving slowly, still has far to go to be really attractive. Many thoughtful observers estimate that Middle Eastern private investors still, as they have for many years, put more capital to work in the West than do Western investors in the Middle East.

Fifth, compared to other catalysts at work, economic and technical assistance from the West—offered via Point Four, U.N. programs and British undertakings—has proved to be of minor consequence. Iraq, Kuwait, Saudi Arabia, Syria, Lebanon and Egypt have, until recently, had only modest assistance. Aid to Jordan has been much more substantial, but resource shortages and overpopulation have made the job a line-holding one—not a boost into take-off. Political problems besetting both donor and recipient nations have joined to keep foreign economic aid from really having a try so far in the Arab East. Meanwhile technical assistance is offered, to the strident accompaniment of its supporters and critics. The former point to the advances made by aid programs in agricultural extension and several other fields. Others decry the large staffs and office buildings full of transplanted bureaucrats who draw, say the critics, their basic intellectual sustenance from the writings of Professor Parkinson. In the Arab East, assistance to governments has certainly not played the role that it did earlier in Western Europe, and has possibly played more recently in Turkey and Israel—where grants have been more substantial.

Next, the Arab East is now engulfed in a series of national economic plans. Iraq, Syria, Egypt and Jordan have them, and even Saudi Arabia and Lebanon—longtime citadels of laissez-faire—now seem intent at least on producing documentary outlines for public expenditure. So does Libya. These all derive from the emergence of military governments, the increasingly widespread belief that any respectable country has a five-year plan (and a steel mill), massive revenues in the hands of governments, increasing numbers of young men returning home with college degrees in economics earned abroad, and a growing abandonment of faith in the price system as allocator of resource in the underdeveloped areas. All this indicates a vigor, while it also raises many painful questions. To date, the successes of planning in the Arab East are hard indeed to define, and probably consist largely of improvement of the education of Western advisors as to dimensions of the problem.

Seventh, reform of the basis of agriculture has only begun in the Arab East and cannot yet be said to have gained lasting momentum. Using Egypt's plan as prototype, Syria and Iraq have initiated publicly-supported land redistribution schemes. More than an occasional "improving landlord" in Lebanon and Syria offers chances for nearby peasants to learn better techniques under private auspices. Yet nothing resembling a family-sized farm concept has been shaped, the area's economists are in wide disagreement over whether cotton acreage should be increased or cut—in Egypt and elsewhere—and most Arab countries are beset with the standard Islamic East burden of overconcentration of ownership mixed with overfragmented holdings. Although this is changing rapidly throughout the area, the components which will lead to increased rural output and purchasing power are only in the earliest stages of assembly.

Next, industry in the Arab East has as yet shown virtually

no capacity to "add value" and compete for markets in the outside world. The industry which has developed—and growth has been rapid since 1940 in Lebanon and Syria and more recently in Egypt—has aimed at creating substitutes for imports. Like nearby Turkey and Israel, Arab East manufacturing plants have had great difficulty breaking the hermetic seal created by expensive raw materials, power costs, problems of management and supervision and limited domestic purchasing power. After a postwar upsurge, industry throughout the Arab East has about held its own since 1945. It cannot yet be said to have expanded its proportionate role in the structure of the over-all economy.

Further, countries of the Arab East have sunk, each year since World War II, a growing percentage of national incomes into armament expenditures. Again as in neighboring Iran, Turkey and Israel, these now total close to 10 per cent of national income in most countries. Such expenditures represent a real competition to those which might go toward economic development. And few Arab armies have been noted for providing basic education or mechanical training to citizen soldiers. Recently, Soviet aid has relieved the burden on domestic resources somewhat, but, regardless, that burden remains far too high.

Next, one may venture the admittedly subjective judgment that the Arab East's reservoir of intellectual skill and technology is not increasing rapidly enough to overcome the problems posed by burgeoning population (almost 3 per cent yearly according to most estimates), defense budget wastes and limitations posed by paucity of resources. In the West the big advances over time are attributable in large part to education and technological improvement. In the Arab East, education budgets are rising, but a vigorous, all-out investment in human resources has yet to begin. And far too much of college-level academic work remains essentially escapist and unadapted to the peculiar conditions of the area—this is particularly true in the field of economics.

Next, several Arab East countries seem intent on continuing

the economic version of "positive neutralism" through various relationships with the Soviet Union—trade agreements, development loans, oil-drilling contracts, technical assistance. The results of this collaboration, while still hard to assess, suggest that the Soviet Union has gained some advantage through its "stringless" loans, its cotton deals and its willingness to tweak the tail of the West at crucial moments. The arrangements have also created some disillusionment—particularly where overt political activity has accompanied them. On balance it would seem that Soviet aid to date has proved little but that its donors are as inept as we Westerners at finding lasting formulas for success with the undertakings.

Finally, regional cooperation between states in the Arab East has to date proved largely a verbal exercise. There are a few customs agreements and bilateral trading schemes. But to date, no currencies are linked (not even those of Egypt and Syria), transfer of public monies from oil-producing states to "have-not" countries has not evolved, oil-producing countries have proved incapable of getting together to deal collectively with the oil companies, oil transit countries have been unable for three years to agree on division of the fifty-fifty profit split offered by the Trans-Arabian Pipeline Company. Compared to the Arab East today, problems of economic cooperation besetting the Common Market and the "Outer Seven" in Europe seem disarmingly simple.

So much for the obvious patterns. To reduce it all to defensible forecasts is impossible. So I shall close with a set of suggestions which can best be categorized as wild speculation. These are:

1. The economic outlook is, with some exceptions, essentially favorable.

2. So long as Middle East oil flows Westward, the substantial increases in national and per capita incomes seem destined to continue—despite competition between North African and Middle Eastern oil.

3. Rapid population growth and overburdensome arms

budgets will soon pose real problems to the area's intellectual infrastructure.

4. The Soviet Union will be an increasingly eager participant in Arab East economic development—and as the West has found, this eagerness may not always yield Russia the desired results.

5. Economic development will remain largely a national matter. Meanwhile, interminable conferences on the subject of regional economic integration will go on—to the intense satisfaction of hotelkeepers, airline operators and those who write the hernia-provoking stacks of economic intelligence letters now emanating from Beirut, Cairo and London.

For details of the problems and issues condensed in this study, the reader is referred to the following books and articles:

Allen, R. L., *Middle Eastern Economic Relations with the Soviet Union, Eastern Europe and Mainland China* (Charlottesville, Virginia, 1958).

Badre, Albert, "National Income of Lebanon," *Middle East Economic Papers, 1956* (Beirut, 1957).

Berliner, Joseph S, *Soviet Economic Aid* (New York, 1958).

Calamitsis, Evangelos, *"Postwar Trends in Egypt's Foreign Trade."* Unpublished M. A. dissertation. (Stanford University, 1955).

Fenelon, K. G., *Iraq's National Income and Expenditure, 1950-1956* (Baghdad, 1958).

Finnie, David, *Desert Enterprise* (Cambridge, Mass., 1958).

Institute for Mediterranean Affairs, *The Palestine Refugee Problem* (New York, 1958).

Lubbell, Harold, *Israel's National Expenditures, 1950-1954* (Jerusalem, 1958).

Meyer, A. J., *Middle Eastern Capitalism* (Cambridge, Mass., 1959).

United Nations, *Commodity Trade Statistics, II-IV,* 1952-1956.

United Nations, *Economic Developments in the Middle East 1956-1957* (New York, 1958).

United Nations, *The Development of Manufacturing Industry in Egypt, Israel and Turkey* (New York, 1958).

United Nations Relief Works Administration, *The Economic Development Projects of Syria* (Beirut, 1958).

Generations, Classes and Politics, 1952-1959

by

William R. Polk

William R. Polk is Assistant Professor of
Semitic Languages and History and a mem-
ber of the staff of the Center for Middle
Eastern Studies at Harvard University.

The approach to another culture is in essence an aesthetic experience. The interpreter can never record the full range of reality but must reach into the culture to select a single facet, or at best a handful of what to him are crucial factors, with which to explain the whole. This process, of course, involves distortions. The distortions can be "artistic" or merely grotesque, but they are always distortions. This is not to say that the selection of a single point or a few points is not useful. Indeed, it is necessary in *any* description of *any* event. But in using an arbitrary selection of this sort, one introduces himself into the very picture he is trying to describe—he is apt to pick what to him (as an outsider) is most striking, must interpret it in terms of his own culture, and will deal with it at least partially in terms of his own experience. Thus, he must constantly have recourse to the context from which he has developed the tools of his analysis.

I have been involved in recent years in my attempt to understand the modern Arab World with just such a concept. The element which has seemed, and still does seem, most useful and most meaningful to me is nationalism. Upon this peg, I have found I could hang, to my greater satisfaction than upon any other, the many-faceted events of recent years. But I can recognize limitations in my own views due both to my own biases and to the changes so rapidly taking place in the area itself. What I should like to do, therefore, is to try to reconsider the context from which I derive nationalism as I understand it, specifically to try to put nationalism into the context of changes in the social structure and the passing of generations.

This sort of reappraisal would be useful under any circumstances, but in the current circumstances of the Middle East it is necessary, for we are not dealing with a coherent body of doctrine, with a developed literature, but rather with what are often unvocalized sentiments, the precise nature of which we must infer from scanty and diffuse evidence. The nature of "nationalism" is thus surely not the same today as it was in 1930, still less 1900. Nor does it embrace the same aims for the men of divergent social and economic means. In the United States we are well aware that, at any given time, generations differ from one another in their values, expectations and activities. What our youth wants is not the same pattern of life desired by their elders. We refer to the "radical" of twenty becoming the "conservative" of forty. But we are also aware of the fact that the frame of reference of the individual, society itself, is in motion, that what the young man of 1900 demanded, his counterpart in 1930 would not accept; that what the man of 1930 wanted, the youth of 1960 would not accept. We can see this in our relatively stable society, but it is difficult for us to realize the extent and depth of the revolution in this social context in the Middle East.

The first factor to stress in any analysis of Arab nationalism is the small portion of the society which it reached until quite recently. On the eve of World War I, the number of Arabs involved in the various secret societies probably was only a few hundred. Many educated and politically active Arabs served on the Ottoman side throughout the war, and in the general disillusionment which came, particularly to Faisal's movement in Syria, in 1919, a resurgence of loyalty to the Ottoman Empire was observable. Nor were the aims of the young nationalists particularly radical or inclusive: what they wanted was self-determination and they hardly considered what they would do with their destiny once they controlled it. They had no coherent body of literature nor much agreement amongst themselves as to what they wanted, who they *were,* or on what principles they would build their future. They could be sure only that they wanted to be left alone. Their attention was directed almost entirely to the outside, to their relations with the mandate powers. With certain modifications, this was a situation which was to continue until the end of World War II.

As one reads the books and pamphlets of the 1920's and 1930's, he can hardly help but be struck by how little attention was paid to the major and startling social changes then taking place in the society. Let us look at Iraq for an example of these.

Two major trends were set in motion in Iraq by World War I. The first of these in point of time was a dislocation of the traditional relationship between people, between the bedouin and his shaikh; the peasant and the tax collector, and the various men of the city and of the three modes of life, bedouin, village, and urban, one to the other. To control rural areas, the British developed a policy begun in the nineteenth century by Ibrahim Pasha in Syria and Medhat Pasha in Iraq, of inducing tribes to settle. Land was provided, seed lent, and a clan chief was promoted, by the Government, to paramount rank over the tribe and was given a subsidy to enable him to effect his control over the tribesmen. As a Report in 1918 put it,

> ". . . Shaikhs . . . certainly without Government support and backing could do nothing . . . our policy has been to force [the tribes] to acknowledge their head shaikhs, refusing to deal with individuals or sections except through the head shaikh."

From what we know of bedouin society, this was a political revolution, for the shaikh had scarcely been more than a generous host and a respected arbitrator to his fellow tribesmen, never their ruler. The social dimensions of this revolution were effected more gradually as the military means of coercion made it possible to impose the urban legal code of the Ottoman Empire over the rural areas. Lands, which had been thought of as tribal or village, which tribesmen and villager had registered in the name of an influential man to escape taxation or military service or over which these men had acquired a "tax farm," acquired a new legal status as their private property. The introduction of the pump, the rise of markets for the export of grain, the failure of the camel market, and the pacification of the rural areas led to widespread settlement and to the enclosing of common lands. The desert ceased to be a reservoir of freedom and the city merchant extended his control into areas which were before that time beyond the reach of Ottoman jurisdiction.

During the period 1920 to 1932, great tracts of land along the Iraqi rivers which had been lightly used by semi-nomadic tribes as grazing, water and winter wheat areas, now became regularly cultivated private property. In 1921, there were 140 pumps on the Iraqi rivers, irrigating about 200 square kilometers; by 1929 over 2,000 pumps irrigated over 7,400 square kilometers. The small farmer, unable to raise the money needed for pumps and unable to defend his customary rights in the new legal concepts of the city, lost out to the new combination of city merchant and tribal shaikh who together invested in lands and pumps and who were able to seize control of the newly created national parliament. By 1933 in Iraq (somewhat earlier in Egypt and later in Syria), this new combination was able to write its actual position into law. In that year, the Iraqi Parliament, now freed of all restraints, passed the "Law Governing the Rights of Cultivators" which contained such provisions as these: no "cultivator" could leave the land if he were in debt, and debt was defined to include all advances of seed, animals or equipment, all work done by the owner, payments on previous debts and any neglect of duties by the peasant. No man in debt was to be employed by any other landlord nor by the government. Even a man dismissed from his job was bound to the land until the end of the planting season, and the landowner was authorized to call upon government force if needed. In short, the tribesman had become a serf; the shaikh, the representative of urban government. And no longer could one escape to the desert because he would be hunted down and brought back by the government even if he could support himself in the now-ruined desert economy. Only the city remained as an escape, and it was at this period that we begin to see the rapid growth of the mud-hut slums about such cities as Baghdad.

The second major trend is the change in the nature of political groups. At the time when the British invaded Iraq, there was no notion of an Iraqi state or nation. The Baghdadi felt no more alien in Damascus than I do in Washington—there were dialectical differences and so forth but no different concept of loyalty. The tribesman thought in terms of his tribe or more accurately his clan, his *qawm*, when one asked him to what he belonged and what he would defend. The villager likewise thought of his village as his *watan*. The city man might mention the district of the city or his craft guild. The Christian might mention his *millet* or religious nation. And the Muslim, facing the challenge of Christian invasion, his *millet*, which was the Ottoman Empire itself. The answer indeed depended, at least partially, on the nature of the question and the source of the question.

For Muslims, it became difficult to answer in Muslim terms. Abdul Hamid's tyranny had driven the Syrian nationalists to Egypt where a split developed between the Egyptian Muslims —who saw the Ottoman Empire in a mist of distance and those who knew it first hand. The compromise was perhaps found in the Islamic Nationalism of Mustafa Kemal. The Young Turk movement destroyed Islam as the political mortar of the Ottoman Empire. Indeed, by the 1931 Jerusalem Congress, Islam was openly regarded as simply "a religious shield" for the Arabs. For Christians, a religious answer to the question of national identity was unsatisfactory in that it necessarily put them outside of the main stream of political life of the area. Thus, before World War I, both Muslims and Christians—in the very small numbers involved in the anti-Ottoman agitation—began searching for another concept by which to define themselves. Two such concepts were available: one was linguistic and cultural, Arabism, which by predating Islam at one blow offered a solution to the

Sunni-Shi'i splits within Islam and to Muslim-Christian antagonism. A second was territorial and also offered an end to religious
feuding. The latter concept was underwritten by the awareness
of a distant past in Egypt, in particular, as shown for example in
the works of such writers as Taha Hussein. In Lebanon, a Phoeni-
cian image was accepted, particularly by the Maronites, while in
Iraq relics of the pre-Islamic past also exerted a vague influence.
These tendencies were strengthened by the Mandate creation of
separate nation-states.

"State building" was the theme of the 1920's. What it
involved was the superficial imposition of an administration and
a set of laws on a territory. For example, events of the war led
to the creation of the British Mandate of Iraq, composed of the
old *villayets* of Basra, Baghdad and Mosul. No longer was it
possible for the "Iraqi" to travel easily to French-mandated Syria:
a passport was required. Jobs were available in the Iraqi services,
and to these flocked the educated and semi-educated inhabitants.
Customs of service were imposed, largely on the model of British
India, to which officials grew accustomed, and these created attitudes which were not held by Syrian Arabs holding comparable
jobs in Damascus. Differences of approach also developed between Iraq and Jordan, which, although also within the British
sphere, drew its administrative traditions from Egyptian rather
than Indian experience. Dialectical differences in language were
supplemented by differences in technical terminology. The Iraqi
army manuals—say, on automobile repair—could hardly be
understood by the Syrian, Jordanian or Egyptian. Local busi-
nesses developed English sources of supply, English methods of
commercial activity, etc., which were different from those of the
Syrian. And, of no small importance, the Iraqi on a visit to Syria
found that his enemies were not shared: whereas he was apt to
feel that the massive, awe-inspiring goblin of British intelligence
was the sole force between him and complete independence, his
Syrian counterpart held an opposite view. The brief period of
Anglo-Arab rule in Syria was recalled with some fondness

whereas the French, against whom the Iraqi felt no antagonism, were hated, feared and emulated.

And turning from the underlying social and political changes, the nature of the literate elite itself was changing. The "people who counted" in Iraq in 1920 were a few score; all the cabinets from 1921 to 1933 were drawn from only two score men; but the extension of education, begun very gradually under the British Mandate, was accelerating. In 1921, only 3.03 per cent of the Iraqi budget was spent on education, with 0.6 per cent of the population registered in schools. British policy was to restrict education to the "select few." It was not until 1920 that secondary schools were opened: one in Baghdad with seven students and one in Mosul with twenty-seven, of whom the majority were Christian. The function of the secondary schools was said by the Government to be "to select and train leaders for all the essential phases of the life of the nation." By the end of the mandate period, the number of pupils in secondary schools had reached about 2,000—an impressive growth but a number which was less impressive in comparison with the whole population. Significantly, education was the first ministry to be taken over by the Iraqis, and from then on the spread of education, though not the rise of standards, was impressive. By 1940-1956, secondary schools contained 14,000 students.

Education was a key factor in the process of "nation-building." The aim of teaching history was to "strengthen the 'national and patriotic feeling' in the hearts of the pupils." A thorough grounding in classical Arabic poetry was considered essential, and the essence of Arabic cultural ethics, fixed in the corpus of Arabic literature, was drilled into a steadily widening circle of society. Where possible, the "nation-building" aspects of education were underwritten by the organized activities of the Boy Scouts or other paramilitary organizations. These were looked upon as preliminary military training programs while the Army itself, really a giant school in basic skills, was used as a means of "fostering a true national spirit." But there was much resistance to this national spirit. As an American educator wrote in 1932, "Without a public school system, it is obvious to everyone that an independent nationality could not be maintained even if established . . . [but even in the schools] there is evident no great patriotic fervor for their new nationalism."

The attention of youth was ever directed to foreign affairs; this is, of course, most strikingly the case on the Right Wing and there particularly so in the *Futuwah* movement which was begun in 1935. Its aim was to accustom the youth "to roughness and to induce patriotic sentiments." It was the fear of alien political control which motivated the initiators of the *Futuwah* movement, but no less directed to foreign affairs was the left wing, as was shown, also in 1935, by the publication of the first fruit of the contact of Iraqi students with Western universities, a well-documented study of British interests in Iraq. In the same year was founded a club to foster pan-Arab activities and to concentrate attention on Palestine. These sentiments were echoed in Syria in the first pan-Arabist conference, at Bludan (Syria) in 1937. And finally, the Rashid Ali coup d'état precipitated foreign relations into a crisis, leading to a British invasion and the enforced withdrawal of Iraqis from foreign affairs except along certain narrowly restricted lines.

The war served, to a limited extent, to divert attentions to domestic issues and, just at the end of the war, one finds in Iraq for the first time two political parties whose policy was essentially directed toward domestic affairs; but almost before domestic issues could begin to compete for the minds of men, the events in Palestine demanded and got the attention of the most active and influential Arab politicians. All politically active Arabs— holding whatever brand of nationalism—had accepted Palestine as their first major challenge, and the failure there, a failure which could not be hidden, was itself the factor which concentrated the attention of thinking men on domestic affairs.

There were attempts to explain away the Palestine defeat as merely the "legacy of the widespread domination of the Middle

East by Western powers . . . it was imperialism's last fling." But few would or could accept this as the central cause. As Constantine Zurayq wrote, Palestine involved

> . . . a collapse of values . . . the doubt of the Arabs in their governments . . . and leaders . . . and in themselves and in their potentiality as a nation.

As Anwar Sadat wrote,

> The humiliation, frustration and anger aroused by the incompetence of the men who had led Egypt to defeat instead of victory, provoked a passionate desire to overthrow a régime which had once again its complete incompetence.

And as one reads the press and other writings about the years 1950-1952, he cannot help but be struck by the constancy of demands for a total re-evaluation of the social fabric and a "fundamental transformation of Arab life."

Against what standards, one should ask, were these demands being made? And here we must return briefly to education. I should now like to mention the rôle of education abroad with the consequent exposure to Western life. To take Iraq again, in 1921-1922, nine Iraqis were sent abroad to study; by 1928-1929, the number had risen to ninety-three; by 1939-1940, it reached 238. By 1931, over 200 had gone abroad, and by 1950 the number was about 2,000. As the Development Board in Iraq devoted funds to these missions, numbers increased, and as they did, the social groups from which the young men and women were drawn widened also. And, perhaps most significantly, whereas education in Iraq involved an exposure to the West in an Eastern context, a student on mission abroad might spend upwards of eight years living in the West, acquiring its habits of life, and, upon his return, naturally would become extremely critical of what he found. As one young man put it,

> It is our contact with the outside world which makes this young generation feel responsible for something which did

not exist for my father's or my grandfather's generation. We feel a personal duty to accomplish things which will make our society respectable in the eyes of the world.

Curiously, this sort of impact seems to have come more strongly as one descends the social ladder. Perhaps it was partly that the young man from a humble family could more fully throw himself into the new life and also, upon his return, more bitterly felt his old position.

And returning to Iraq, the professionally trained young man had to work for the Government—a government he blamed for Palestine and to whom he gave no loyalty. He was required to do so to pay for his education, but in most fields government work was the only possible employment. The professions were all intermixed with government service. For example, a doctor virtually had to work part-time for a government agency—I have been told that the allocation of time might be something like this: as a government doctor, a man might see up to a hundred patients in the morning but only four or five in his afternoon private clinic: essentially he was a government employee. Engineers usually worked in government departments or in companies on whose boards sat government representatives. And, of course, the great bulk of returning students became teachers. But regardless of what one did, he fell under the scrutiny of the government and felt his job threatened by any political expression on his own part. Thus, it was normal for him to impose upon himself a censorship more rigorous than that imposed or perhaps wanted by the Government. But the crucial factor is this: he blamed the government not only for its weakness and failures but also for his own.

Meanwhile the rapid rise of investment, the creation of many new "social overhead" facilities, and the wide publication of plans and programs led to a rapid rise in expectations—if it *were* possible to improve the standard of living, why was this not also possible to do rapidly and in depth. It could hardly be otherwise than this: expectations far outran performance. One might almost say that the better the government in economic terms, the worse it became in political terms. To get on with the job, Nuri Pasha Sa'id had stifled all criticism and opposition and had turned into covert fear and hatred what might otherwise have expressed itself openly and positively as constructive criticism.

When the blow came in Iraq, it was (as in Egypt) from the army officer corps, a group repeatedly purged since the 1930's —when it had taken a key part in the rise and fall of governments. Constant purging had kept the corps weak, but also had kept it young, and the officers who came to the fore after the July 14 coup were mostly of the postwar generation. We lack any statistics or studies on them as yet, but it is clear that many are also men of the "lower middle class" and this leads me to a point about which I am still unsure but which could explain something of the intellectual changes of recent years in Iraq— that is, the social implications of the educational divisions in recent years.

The young men who went abroad to study in the 1930's were often men "of family." To have got into a position to profit by years abroad, one already had to have made a considerable investment in education, and this was possible for only a thin stratum of the population. With the rapid extension of primary and secondary education in the 1930's and 1940's, however, this ceased to be entirely the case. And people of lesser means came to benefit from higher education. Here a new social division was created: those who stayed in Iraq for their study could not be given and were not given professional tools comparable to that which their counterparts got in Europe or America. The graduate of the Baghdad colleges was destined for an inferior job—he might be a primary or secondary schoolteacher—whereas the man who studied abroad could teach in the colleges, practice his profession, or go into responsible government positions. He had considerable chance to enrich himself. Furthermore, while abroad

he became particularly conscious of himself as an Arab. In
Europe or America, he was sensitive to the fact that he was
alien, and he drew close to other Arabs, from whatever country.
Let me take one example.

In 1938, a group of Arab students resident in Europe held
a meeting at Brussels and subsequently published their proceedings. The opening page of their book deals with the crucial question of identification: Who are we? The term Arab, not Iraqi or
Muslim or Syrian, is chosen, for it alone gives a common bond
to the diverse group. Arab is defined as "everyone who is Arab
in language, culture and *wila'*," the latter term being defined in
a footnote as one who has "nationalist sentiments—*ash-Shu'ur
al Qawmi.*" *Qawmiyah* or nationalism is subsequently defined
as "sensitivity to the existing necessity of liberating and unifying
the inhabitants of the Arab lands in view of the unity of the
watan (territory) and language and culture and history, and
[the necessity] of improving those things which are a common
concern."

Now, the young man who lacked this exposure abroad had
not been challenged, by foreigners, in his Arabism and could not
but feel a sense of apartness from the few other Arabs he met. He
was amused at the Egyptian accent in the cinema, spoke with
disdain about the Saudi Arab or Palestinian refugee and had
turned his attention much more fixedly on the domestic evils
which particularly affected those who became, as he might,
rural schoolteachers. He, not the man educated abroad, was
particularly sensitive to the social revolution which I have described above, and thus I would generalize from the several score
individuals I know and say that he was more concerned with
what you might call "social nationalism" than with pan-Arabism.

Both the man educated abroad and the local student were
alike in their demand that the old ruling class, the class responsible for Palestine, must go. But upon achieving the destruction
of the old order, their differences rapidly came to the fore in
Iraq. Neither is concerned with representative government, with

which both associated the power of tribal shaikhs, opportunists and vested interests. Both believe in the rôle of the army as the efficient, reforming agent of power. But between them is a profound difference on the basic question of identification: Of what territory, people, and culture is one to be a nationalist?

The issue is still in doubt.

Index
of Names
and Places

'Abbas, Farhat, 89
'Abd al-Nasir, Col. (see Nasir)
'Abd al-Qadir, Prince, 94
Abdul Hamid, 111
Abdul Raziq, 53
Aden, 44
Aden, Gulf of, 67
Africa, 65, 66, 67, 68, 70, 74, 75, 76, 77, 78, 79, 80, 81, 82
African continent, the, 71
Ahijo, Ahmadu, Prime Minister, 73, 74
Aksum (Ethiopia), 66
Alexandria, 23, 31, 43
Algeria, 87, 90, 91, 92, 98, 99
Algiers, 90
Almohades, 90
Almoravids, 66, 90
America (see United States)
Anglo-Egyptian Treaty (1954), 32
Arab Development Bank, 37
Arabian peninsula, 44, 45, 67
Arab League, 30, 37, 88
Argentina, 91
Asyut, 43
Awolowo, 74
'Ayn Shams, 43
Azerbaijan, 35
Ashar, the, 43
Azikwe, 74

Baghdad, 43, 88, 111, 112, 113, 117
Baghdad Pact, 32
Bamileke (tribesmen), 73
Basra (Basrah), 88, 112

Belgian Congo, 65, 70, 81
Berber communities, 66
Berber dynasties, 90
Beirut, 31, 32, 43, 50, 103
Bergue, Jacques, 21
Bilad as-Sudan, 66
Bludan (Syria), 114
Bourguiba (Burqibah), Habib, 89, 93
Britain, 33, 34, 35
British Commonwealth, 93
British India, 112
British Royal Air Force, 32
Brussels, 118

Caffrey, Jefferson, 32
Cairo, 31, 43, 103
Cameroun Republic, 73, 74, 82
Canal Zone, 32, 33
Casablanca, 87, 88
Castile, 66
Central African Republic, 82
Chad, 72, 73, 82
Churchill, Winston, 33
Common Market, 102
Convention People's Party (CPP), 76
Cyrenaica, 87

Dahomey, 82
Damascus, 32, 43, 94, 111, 112
"Dark Continent," 65
Development Board (Iraq), 115
Dia, Mamadou, 75, 80
Douala, 73

East Africa, 66
Eastern Mediterranean, 35
Egypt, 29, 30, 31, 32, 33, 34, 35, 38,
   39, 40, 41, 42, 43, 44, 51, 59, 87,
   90, 91, 97, 98, 99, 100, 101, 102,
   110, 111, 112, 115, 117
England, 35
Entente, the (Niger, Dahomey, Up-
   per Volta, Ivory Coast), 82
Equatorial Africa (Gabon, Came-
   roun, Chad, Central African Re-
   public), 82
Ethiopia, 66
Euphrates, 29, 98
Europe, 56, 65, 118

Faisal, King, 108
France, 29, 33, 35, 38, 73, 90, 91,
   92, 94
French Africa, 76
French Community, 76
French Equatorial Africa, 81
French West Africa, 70
French West African Federation, 72
Fulani, 68, 69, 73
Futa Jalon, 79
Futuwah movement, 114

Gandhi, (Mahatma), 34
Gaulle, Charles de, 76, 92
Ghana, 76, 77
Ghazi, 19
Ghazzali, al, 53
Gibraltar, 33
Goethe (Johann Wolfgang), 60
Great Britain, 33, 38
Guinea, 72, 76, 77, 78, 81

Hadramawt, 44
"High Dam," 17
Hikma University, 43
Hodgkin, Thomas, 80
Horn area, 70, 82
Houphouet-Boigny, Felix, 75
Husayn, Ahmad, 43

Husayn dynasty, 93
Husayn, King, 32
Hussein, Taha, 53, 112

Ibo, 74
Ibn Khaldun, 53
Ibn Rushd, 53
Ibn Yasin, 66
Ibrahim Pasha, 109
Imam of Muscat, 67
India, 41
Indonesia, 41
Iran, 101
Iraq, 29, 30, 32, 35, 36, 38, 39, 40,
   41, 42, 44, 57, 59, 88, 109, 110,
   111, 112, 113, 114, 115, 116,
   117, 118
Iraqi Parliament, 110
Islamic East, 100
Israel, 30, 34, 36, 37, 49, 77, 100,
   101
Istiqlal party, 90
Ivory Coast, 81, 82

Jerusalem, 37
Jerusalem Congress, 1931, 111
Jihad, 68
Jordan, 30, 31, 32, 34, 38, 42, 97,
   98, 99, 100, 112

Kemal, Mustafa, 19, 111
Kenya, 67, 70
Khartum, 43
Koulamallah, Ahmad, 72
Kuwait, 97, 98, 99

League of Arab States, 37
Lebanese University, 43
Lebanon, 31, 32, 33, 34, 35, 38, 42,
   44, 52, 53, 97, 98, 99, 100, 101,
   112
Levant, 98
Libya, 87, 98, 99, 100
London, 103
London Conference (First), 41

Macmillan, Sir Harold, 65
Madagascar, 90
Maghrib, 87, 88, 89, 90, 91, 93, 94
Malagasy Republic, 65
Mali, 65, 66, 72, 80, 82
Malta, 33
Maronites, 112
Marrakesh, 90
Marx (Karl), 55
Mau Mau, 65
Mauritania, 66, 72, 87
Massignon, Louis, 16
Mecca, 80
Medhat Pasha, 109
Métropole, 92
Middle East, 19, 29, 30, 33, 35, 36,
    41, 42, 43, 61, 99, 102, 108, 115
Millet, 111
Mills, C. Wright, 81
Misr Bank, 30
Mombasa, 67
Moors, 72
Morocco, 87, 88, 90, 91, 93, 98
"Morocco Irredenta," 90
Mosul, 112, 113
Mozambique, 70, 81
Muhammad Abdu, 53
Muhammad Ali, 29
Muhammad V, King, 87, 88, 90,
    93, 94
Muhammad (Prophet), 13, 53, 66
Muslim Association Party, 76
Muslim Brotherhood, 40, 51
Muslim Emirates, 68
Muslim Emirs, 68
Mu'tazilites, 53

Nadel, S. F., 68, 69
Naguib, General, 40
Nahas Pasha, 57
Nasir (of Egypt), 19, 38, 40, 41, 42
National Liberation Front (FLN),
    88, 89, 91, 92, 94
National Political Bureau, 78
Near East, 82

New York (City), 92
Niasse, El Hadj Ibrahim (Grand
    Marabout of Kaloack), 79
Nietzsche (Friedrich), 59
Niger, 72, 82, 90
Nigeria, 66, 68, 69, 70, 74, 91
Nile Valley, 66
Nkrumah, Kwame (Prime Minis-
    ter), 75, 76
North Africa, 59, 87, 90
Nupe, 68, 69
Nyere, Julius, 75

Ottoman Empire, 29, 35, 108, 109,
    111
Outer Seven, 102

Palestine, 30, 39, 40, 87, 114, 115,
    116, 118
Pan-Arabism, 118
Pan-Arabist conference, 1937, 114
Parkinson (Professor), 99
Parti de la Solidarité Senegalaise
    (PSS), 79, 80
Parti Democratique de Guinée
    (PDG), 78, 79, 80, 81
Parti National Africain (PNA), 72
Parti Progressiste Tchadien (PPT-
    RDA), 73
Persian Gulf, 44, 87
Plato, 55
Point Four, 99

Qawm, 111
Qawmiyah, 118
Qur'an, 13, 17

Rashid Ali, 114
Red Sea, 66
Russia, 29, 35, 103

Sadat, Anwar, 115
Sahara, 70, 80, 81, 82
Sahara, Spanish, 87
Sa'id, Nuri as, Pasha, 57, 117

St. Louis de Sénégal, 87
Sallum, 87
San Francisco, 92
Saudi Arabia, 38, 43, 97, 99, 100
Sayyid Sa'id, Imam, 67
Senegal, 79, 80
Senegal River, 66, 72
Senegambia, 82
Seville, 90
Sharabi, Dr. (Hisham), 24
Shari'a, 13, 14, 17
Shari'a law, 68, 69
Sierra Leone, 81
Singapore, 33
Sixth Fleet, 35
Spain, 90
Somalia, 65
Songhai, 66
South Africa, 65
Soviet Union, 35, 41, 102, 103
Sudan, 31, 33, 38, 39, 40, 44, 59, 72
Sufi, 13, 53
Suez, 35, 40, 41, 98
Syria, 31, 32, 33, 34, 38, 39, 40, 41,
    42, 44, 91, 97, 98, 99, 100, 101,
    102, 108, 110, 112, 114

Tajdid, 22
Tanganyika, 67, 70, 81
Tangier Convention, 89, 90, 93
Tangiers, 50
Toucouleurs (Takrur), 72
Tidjani, Cheikh, 80
Tigris, 29, 98
Tivaouane, 80
Touré, Sekou, President, 75, 76, 77,
    78
Trans-Arabian Pipeline Company,
    102
Trimingham, J. S., 68

Tripolitania, 87
Tunis, 90
Tunisia, 52, 53, 87, 89, 90, 91, 93,
    98
Turkey, 35, 53, 100, 101

Uganda, 70
Ulama, 23
Union des Populations Camerou-
    naise (UPC), 73, 74
Union Progressiste Senegalaise
    (UPS), 79, 80
United Arab Republic (UAR), 38,
    39, 41, 42, 57, 71, 88, 91
United Arab States, 93
United Nations, 70, 97, 99
United States, 33, 35, 36, 37, 91,
    118
Upper Volta, 81, 82

Wafd, 40
Washington (District of Columbia),
    111
Watan, 111, 118
Weber, Max, 49
West Africa, 70, 71
Wilcocks, Sir William, 29
Wolof, 72
World War I, 108, 109, 111
World War II, 98, 101, 109

Yaounde, 73
Yemen, 42
Yoruba, 74
Young Turk movement, 111
Yugoslavia, 41

Zanzibar, 67
Zurayq, Constantine, 115